Post-Traumatic Stress Disorder

Scott Barbour

Diseases and Disorders

ReferencePoint
Press®

San Diego, CA

© 2010 ReferencePoint Press, Inc.

For more information, contact:
ReferencePoint Press, Inc.
PO Box 27779
San Diego, CA 92198
www.ReferencePointPress.com

Picture credits:
Cover: iStockphoto.com
Maury Aaseng: 31–34, 46–48, 62–64, 79–83
AP Images: 10, 13

LIBRARY OF CONGRESS CATALOGING-IN-PUBLICATION DATA

Barbour, Scott, 1963–
  Post-traumatic stress disorder / by Scott Barbour.
     p. cm. — (Compact research)
  Includes index.
  ISBN-13: 978-1-60152-101-9 (hardback)
  ISBN-10: 1-60152-101-4 (hardback)
  1. Post-traumatic stress disorder. 2. Post-traumatic stress disorder—Treatment. I. Title.
  RC552.P67.B363 2009
  616.85'21—dc22

                                                                 2009033216

Contents

Foreword

66 Where is the knowledge we have lost in information? 99

—T.S. Eliot, "The Rock."

As modern civilization continues to evolve, its ability to create, store, distribute, and access information expands exponentially. The explosion of information from all media continues to increase at a phenomenal rate. By 2020 some experts predict the worldwide information base will double every 73 days. While access to diverse sources of information and perspectives is paramount to any democratic society, information alone cannot help people gain knowledge and understanding. Information must be organized and presented clearly and succinctly in order to be understood. The challenge in the digital age becomes not the creation of information, but how best to sort, organize, enhance, and present information.

ReferencePoint Press developed the *Compact Research* series with this challenge of the information age in mind. More than any other subject area today, researching current issues can yield vast, diverse, and unqualified information that can be intimidating and overwhelming for even the most advanced and motivated researcher. The *Compact Research* series offers a compact, relevant, intelligent, and conveniently organized collection of information covering a variety of current topics ranging from illegal immigration and deforestation to diseases such as anorexia and meningitis.

The series focuses on three types of information: objective single-author narratives, opinion-based primary source quotations, and facts and statistics. The clearly written objective narratives provide context and reliable background information. Primary source quotes are carefully selected and cited, exposing the reader to differing points of view. And facts and statistics sections aid the reader in evaluating perspectives. Presenting these key types of information creates a richer, more balanced learning experience.

For better understanding and convenience, the series enhances information by organizing it into narrower topics and adding design features that make it easy for a reader to identify desired content. For example, in *Compact Research: Illegal Immigration*, a chapter covering the economic impact of illegal immigration has an objective narrative explaining the various ways the economy is impacted, a balanced section of numerous primary source quotes on the topic, followed by facts and full-color illustrations to encourage evaluation of contrasting perspectives.

The ancient Roman philosopher Lucius Annaeus Seneca wrote, "It is quality rather than quantity that matters." More than just a collection of content, the *Compact Research* series is simply committed to creating, finding, organizing, and presenting the most relevant and appropriate amount of information on a current topic in a user-friendly style that invites, intrigues, and fosters understanding.

Post-Traumatic Stress Disorder at a Glance

Definition

The term *post-traumatic stress disorder*, also commonly known as PTSD, refers to an anxiety disorder that some people get after witnessing or experiencing a traumatic event. An anxiety disorder is a mental illness in which the sufferer feels an exceptional level of fear and apprehension.

Prevalence

According to the Institute of Medicine, 7.8 percent of Americans will experience PTSD at some point during their lifetime. The rate of PTSD among women is at least twice that of men, at 10.4 percent and 5 percent, respectively.

Veterans with PTSD

The latest estimate is that about 14 percent of veterans of the wars in Iraq and in Afghanistan have PTSD. Only about half of them seek treatment, and only half of those who seek treatment receive the optimal level of care.

Signs and Symptoms

There are three types of symptoms of PTSD: reexperiencing symptoms, including flashbacks and nightmares about the traumatic event; avoidance/numbing symptoms, including an avoidance of thinking or talking about the traumatic event; and hyperarousal symptoms, including insomnia, angry outbursts, and difficulty concentrating.

Causes

Scientists have found that the regions of the brain controlling fear and memory are different in people with PTSD. Genetics may also play a role. In addition, people who experience more traumas over a longer period of time are more likely to get PTSD.

Precipitating Traumatic Events

Any event that causes a person to experience intense fear, horror, or help-lessness can lead to PTSD. Exposure to combat is the leading cause of PTSD among American men; assault and rape are the leading causes of the disorder among American women.

Treatment

The main treatments for PTSD are medication and psychotherapy. The most commonly used medications are a type of antidepressant known as selective serotonin reuptake inhibitors (SSRIs). The most commonly used therapy is exposure therapy, in which the patient reexperiences the trauma in a safe setting.

Long-Term Prognosis

One-third of people with PTSD never recover. Most of the remaining two-thirds recover with or without treatment, although they recover more quickly with treatment.

Overview

In August 2005 Hurricane Katrina ripped through the Gulf Coast of the United States, killing more than 1,800 people, displacing over a million, and causing over $100 billion in damage. However, the devastation did not end when the floodwaters receded. Survivors continued to suffer mental health problems resulting from the disaster for months and years. In April 2006, 8 months after the storm, journalist Rukmini Callimachi described the experience of one 14-year-old girl, whose name was withheld to protect her identity:

> The girl . . . used to lose herself in books. Now, she has a hard time concentrating. Horrible images intrude as she reads. She remembers the drowned man, impaled on his plywood fence. She pictures her favorite skirt high up in the branches of a tree. Last month, she locked herself in the bathroom . . . and lifted a bottle of Lysol to her lips.

Her mother found her passed out on the toilet seat. . . . To this girl, the world is a tunnel of darkness. She sees no way out. "It's like I can't see my future anymore," she said.[1]

This girl is suffering from post-traumatic stress disorder, a severe, debilitating mental illness that affects millions of people worldwide.

What Is Post-Traumatic Stress Disorder?

Post-traumatic stress disorder, also commonly known as PTSD, is an anxiety disorder that some people get after witnessing or experiencing a violent, disturbing, or extremely frightening event. The event is typically one that involves a real or threatened injury or death and causes feelings of extreme fear, helplessness, or horror. Most people who experience a trauma have some level of anxiety afterward. Anxiety is a condition in which a person is constantly worried about everyday things and is fearful for no apparent reason. For most people, the anxiety that results from a traumatic event eases with time. However, some people continue to suffer from anxiety months or even years after the event. If the anxiety interferes with their ability to function—that is, to do well in school, hold down a job, and maintain friendships and other social connections—they may have PTSD.

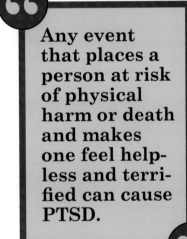

Any event that places a person at risk of physical harm or death and makes one feel helpless and terrified can cause PTSD.

What Are the Causes of PTSD?

Any event that places a person at risk of physical harm or death and makes one feel helpless, terrified, or horrified can cause PTSD. Perhaps the most well-known cause of PTSD is combat. One study found that as many as 14 percent of troops returning from Iraq and Afghanistan suffer from the disorder. Another found that more than 18 percent of Vietnam veterans experienced PTSD at some point after their service.

Other causes of the disorder include natural disasters such as earthquakes, tsunamis, hurricanes, tornadoes, and fires. Acts of mass violence such as warfare, ethnic cleansing, terrorism, and workplace and school shootings can cause symptoms of the disorder. Rates of PTSD are high among people who are displaced from their homes in war-torn regions or who are detained or tortured as political prisoners. Many people who experience physical, sexual, or even emotional abuse as children develop PTSD symptoms that can last throughout their adult lives. Violent crimes such as assault and rape and accidents such as car crashes can also cause PTSD.

In the midst of fighting, a U.S. Marine carries a seriously wounded comrade to safety in Iraq. Many soldiers relive the terrors of war when they return home. One study found that 14 percent of veterans of the wars in Iraq and Afghanistan suffer from PTSD.

The Body's Reaction to Danger

Stress is a normal reaction to a traumatic event, but most people who experience a severe trauma do not develop PTSD. Researchers are not certain why some people are able to move on after trauma while others are haunted for months, years, and even decades. Psychologist Laurie B. Slone and psychiatrist Matthew J. Friedman point out that PTSD is "*not* a sign of weakness. Many people who are brave or strong end up with PTSD."[2]

Most agree that the cause of PTSD starts with the body's reaction to danger. Faced with the threat of death or serious injury, human beings experience a fight-or-flight response that is designed to help them survive. Psychologist Kendall Johnson explains the mechanism of this reaction: "During a crisis . . . our bodies shift almost instantly to survival mode. Blood is directed to major muscle groups. Our heart, respiratory, and blood pressure rates increase. Emotions directly drive our thinking and responding." Johnson goes on to describe the benefits of this reaction. "The fight-or-flight emergency response allows us to quickly prepare our body for survival reactions, focus only on survival-relevant factors, [and] feel pain less acutely."[3]

> " Researchers are not certain why some people are able to move on after trauma while others are haunted for months, years, and even decades. "

The key to PTSD seems to lie in the cascade of chemicals that floods the brain during this moment of heightened experience. For reasons that are not completely clear, in some people memories of the event continue to recur and to reawaken the intense fear—and even the physical sensations—that the person experienced at the time of the event.

Some researchers posit that genetics plays a role in PTSD. People with PTSD may possess a genetic makeup that makes it more difficult to forget painful events. Another theory suggests that the cause lies with the structure of the patient's brain. Perhaps the section of the brain involved in memory is built to hold on to memories that would best be forgotten.

Other researchers focus on potential environmental factors that might make a person susceptible to the disorder. For example, a history of child abuse or mental illness could leave a person vulnerable to the detrimental effects of trauma. In addition, the nature and severity of the trauma may play a role: The more serious the trauma and the longer its duration, the more likely it is that PTSD will result. Most likely, a combination of factors—including both genetic and environmental influences—is responsible for causing the disorder.

The Prevalence of PTSD

Estimates of the number of Americans who suffer from PTSD vary widely depending on the definition of the disorder and the method used to gather the statistics. In general, although men experience more traumatic events than women, women suffer from PTSD at 2 to 3 times the rate of men. The most frequently cited study states that about 7.8 percent of Americans will experience PTSD at some point during their lifetime. The rate is about twice as high for women (10.4 percent) as men (5.0 percent). Within any 12-month period, 3.6 percent of Americans (5.2 percent of women and 1.8 percent of men) will suffer from PTSD.

The Symptoms of PTSD

In movies and on television, a person with PTSD is usually depicted as a combat veteran in an everyday situation who suddenly believes he or she is back in the war surrounded by enemies. This scenario is often exaggerated for dramatic effect. Sadly, this stereotype contains an element of truth. Flashbacks are one of the symptoms of PTSD. For example, journalist Dana Hull tells the story of Stephen Edwards, a soldier with the California National Guard, who returned from Iraq in 2005 and was visiting his daughter's elementary school. Hearing the sound of a nail gun, he suddenly dropped to one knee and shouted, "Bravo team . . . On my six, 300 meters, MOVE!"[4] Slowly, he came to understand he was not in Baghdad surrounded by enemies, but in San Jose, California, surrounded by elementary school children.

Flashbacks are the most well-known symptom of PTSD. They belong to one of three classifications of PTSD symptoms—reexperiencing symptoms, in which the person effectively goes through the traumatic event all over again. In addition to flashbacks, the person may also have unwanted images or thoughts that intrude into their minds. While asleep, the person with PTSD may reexperience the event in the form

Surrounded by the debris of a middle school that collapsed in a 2008 earthquake in southwest China, a woman mourns the death of her child. People who live through traumatic events such as earthquakes, tsunamis, and wildfires can develop PTSD.

of bad dreams or nightmares. This symptom often causes people with PTSD to avoid sleep, which can result in fatigue and difficulty functioning while awake. Slone and Friedman describe the effect that reexperiencing symptoms can have on a war veteran with PTSD:

> It's hard to concentrate when you're awake because the memories intrude on your thoughts while you're trying to think about something else. At night, you may wake up in a sweat, your heart pounding, your mind full of rage, fear, or panic because of intense nightmares about things that happened in the war zone. You are constantly on the lookout for reminders that might trigger such memories. . . . When you encounter such reminders, you may become very emotional or your body might react with a pounding heart, profuse sweating, or headache.[5]

The second type of symptom of PTSD—avoidance symptoms—are those that involve people distancing themselves from the traumatic event or from the emotions connected to it. People may stay away from places, events, or objects that remind them of the traumatic experience. They may feel emotionally numb or have strong feelings of guilt, depression, or worry. They may lose interest in activities that they used to enjoy, and they may have trouble remembering the traumatic event. Colby Buzzell, a veteran of Operation Iraqi Freedom, the U.S.-led war in Iraq that began in 2003, describes experiencing symptoms of avoidance, numbing, and lack of interest: "For a year straight after I came back [from Iraq], I hardly ever left my room, and the only walking that I did was to the liquor store and back to numb myself in my room. I found that I was no longer interested in going out. Nothing interested me . . . and I found myself not interested in meeting or talking to new people, either."[6]

> **People with PTSD often experience other mental illnesses along with PTSD, which can make the disorder difficult to diagnose and can complicate treatment.**

The third and final type of symptom of PTSD—hyperarousal symptoms—include being easily startled, feeling tense or on edge, having angry outbursts, and having difficulty sleeping. People with PTSD tend to have these symptoms at all times—not only when they are reminded of the traumatic event. "When you have PTSD, you're on high alert all the time," Slone and Friedman explain. "The adrenaline is pumping and you're constantly on the lookout for dangerous situations. With such a constant state of arousal, you can't sleep, can't concentrate, are very short-tempered, and very jumpy."[7] Obviously, these symptoms can make it very difficult for a person with PTSD to function every day. To be officially diagnosed with PTSD, a person must have at least one reexperiencing symptom, three avoidance symptoms, and two hyperarousal symptoms. These symptoms must have been present for at least one month, and they must be interfering with the person's ability to function at school, at work, and socially.

PTSD Among Young People

Children and teens have many of the same PTSD symptoms as adults. For example, they may reexperience the precipitating traumatic event in flashbacks or dreams and may feel fearful when reminded of the trauma. However, they may have other symptoms as well. Young children may wet the bed even though they have learned how to use the toilet. They may return to thumb sucking and may forget how or be unable to talk, may act out the traumatic event while playing, and may be exceptionally clingy with their parents or other adults. Older children and teens will display symptoms more similar to those of adults. However, they may also become disruptive, destructive, or disrespectful.

> **Post-traumatic stress disorder is most often treated with therapy, medication, or a combination of both.**

An example of the effects of PTSD on young people can be seen in the words of Scarlet Taveras, a student at the High School for Leadership and Public Services, located near the World Trade Center in New York City. Speaking nine months after the terrorist attacks that destroyed the Twin Towers of the World Trade Center and killed more than 2,600 people in her city, she described what she and her fellow students had experienced:

> The lives of many of us have been changed dramatically. One of my friends has moved from a high-rise apartment where she lived on the 17th floor to an apartment on the first floor because the sound of airplanes on the high floors terrorized her every moment. I have seen students go from an A average to a C average. . . . Students at my school, including myself, have seen an increase in anger and aggressive outbursts. Sleepless nights are the norm. Sleeping instead means we have nightmares.[8]

The avoidance, nightmares, sleepless nights, and angry outbursts Taveras describes are all common symptoms of PTSD.

PTSD Combined with Other Disorders

People with PTSD often experience other mental illnesses along with PTSD, which can make the disorder difficult to diagnose and can complicate treatment. According to the Institute of Medicine (IOM), a research organization that studies health issues for the U.S. government, 80 percent of people with PTSD will also have another mental disorder at some point in their lives; 50 percent will have major depression. Among war veterans, 98.8 percent with PTSD will have another disorder, usually depression or alcohol abuse. Experts believe that many people with PTSD—especially if untreated—turn to drugs and alcohol in an attempt to dull their traumatic memories and ease their pain, which in most cases merely compounds their problems.

> "Fewer than one-fourth of PTSD-inflicted veterans are getting quality treatment for their disorder."

Tragically, in addition to abusing drugs and alcohol, people with PTSD too often resort to suicide to end their suffering. According to psychiatrists David Brody and Michael Serby, "In one study, Vietnam veterans with PTSD had a sevenfold greater risk for suicide compared with Vietnam veterans without PTSD."[9]

How Can PTSD Be Treated?

Post-traumatic stress disorder is most often treated with therapy, medication, or a combination of both. Experts do not agree whether therapy is more effective than medication, whether they are equally effective, or whether the effectiveness of the type of treatment varies from individual to individual. For example, in its 2004 treatment guidelines, the American Psychiatric Association states that therapy and medication are both effective at treating PTSD. However, in guidelines published in 2008, the IOM states that there is not enough evidence to prove that medication is effective for PTSD. Moreover, the IOM finds that only one form of therapy has proved to be effective for PTSD. Despite the IOM's reservations, several types of medication and therapy are used to treat the disorder.

The drugs most commonly prescribed to treat PTSD are a type of antidepressant known as a selective serotonin reuptake inhibitor (SSRI). Although these drugs are usually given to people with major depression, they are also used to treat anxiety and are believed to help patients with feelings of hyperarousal and hypervigilance. In addition, patients with PTSD often also experience depression and suicidal thoughts, and SSRIs can help with these symptoms as well. In addition to SSRIs doctors prescribe other types of drugs to their patients with PTSD, including medications designed to combat insomnia, prevent seizures, and ease mood swings.

Therapy for PTSD

Various kinds of therapy are used in the treatment of PTSD, and they often overlap. Most of them fall within the category of cognitive-behavioral therapy (CBT). In CBT the patient is systematically trained to change his or her thinking in order to improve his or her mood. The most common type of CBT used for PTSD is exposure therapy. In this form of therapy, the patient essentially reexperiences the traumatic event through the use of mental imagery, talking, or writing. By going through the event repeatedly with increasing degrees of exposure, the patient is to some degree desensitized to the trauma, and the memories of the event lose their power to arouse extreme avoidance and arousal reactions. As explained by Tori DeAngelis, writing for the American Psychological Association, exposure to the original trauma is "done in a gradual, controlled and repeated manner until the person can evaluate their circumstances realistically and understand they can safely return to the activities in their current lives that they had been avoiding."[10]

How Should Society Help Soldiers with PTSD?

A 2008 study by the Rand Corporation, a highly regarded nonprofit research institution, found that 14 percent of soldiers returning from Iraq and Afghanistan suffered from PTSD and that 303,000 veterans had PTSD or major depression. Moreover, only about half (53 percent) of these veterans sought treatment, and only about half of those who sought it received high-quality treatment. As Rand explains: "Of those who have a mental disorder and also sought medical care for that problem, just over half received minimally adequate treatment. The number who received *quality* care (i.e., a treatment that has been demonstrated to be effective) would be expected to be even smaller"[11] In other words, fewer than one-fourth of PTSD-inflicted veterans are getting quality treatment for their disorder.

In light of Rand's troubling statistics, many politicians and commentators are calling on the government to get help to the veterans who need it. Specifically, experts contend that veterans must be given more encouragement to seek help. To this end, military leaders must confront the prevailing belief in the military that PTSD is a sign of weakness and that soldiers should be able to get over it. In addition, experts say that high-quality treatment must be made more widely available and more easily accessible.

The benefits of treatment for veterans can be seen in the example of Ryan Kahlor, an army sergeant who returned from two tours of duty in Iraq in 2007. As described by David Zucchino, a reporter for the *Los Angeles Times*, upon his return, Kahlor "was diagnosed with post-traumatic stress disorder and traumatic brain injury. He was violent and suicidal. He carried a loaded handgun everywhere. He drank until he passed out. He cut himself. He burned his own skin with cigarettes. He bit through his tongue just to watch himself bleed."[12] In response to repeated prodding by his distressed parents, Kahlor eventually entered a Veteran's Administration treatment program. Today he is planning to enroll in college. His gun is locked in a drawer, and he often speaks to other soldiers, urging them to get treatment for PTSD. Kahlor credits treatment with saving his life. Without it, he says, he would "be sitting in a dark room somewhere—or dead."[13]

Kahlor's story reveals the toll PTSD can take on individuals, their families, and society. PTSD is a devastating illness that leads to extreme distress, driving many people to self-medicate with drugs and alcohol or, even worse, take their own lives. Parents, spouses, and children are left with their own scars as they watch their loved one spiral out of control. However, Kahlor's story also shows that there is hope for people who suffer from the invisible wounds of trauma. With the help of treatment, many of them can bury the demons of the past and go on to lead fulfilling lives.

What Is Post-Traumatic Stress Disorder?

66 Posttraumatic stress disorder is a medically recognized anxiety disorder that can develop in anyone after they've been exposed to extremely stressful situations. 99

—Laurie B. Slone, associate director for research and education at the Veterans Administration National Center for PTSD, and Matthew J. Friedman, executive director of the National Center for PTSD.

66 The majority of people exposed to traumatic events do not develop PTSD. Instead, they might suffer minimal symptoms or short-lived distress before they bounce back to normal functioning. 99

—Richard Ransley, clinical supervisor of the Santa Fe Rape Crisis and Trauma Treatment Center in New Mexico.

P TSD did not become an official psychiatric diagnosis until 1980, when it first appeared in the *Diagnostic and Statistical Manual of Mental Disorders (DSM)*, the American Psychiatric Association's (APA) list of mental illnesses and their symptoms. However, its relatively recent addition to the manual does not mean PTSD is a new condition; rather, PTSD is simply a new name for a disorder that has affected humans throughout history.

Soldiers in all wars have experienced PTSD, although prior to 1980 it was called by different names and poorly understood. In the revolutionary era the condition was referred to as "melancholia" or "insanity." During the American Civil War, it was termed "soldier's heart" or "irritable heart." In World War I, the condition became known as "shell shock." In World War II and Korea, it was called "battle fatigue" or "exhaustion." Vietnam veterans afflicted with the disorder were said to have "post-Vietnam syndrome." As stated by Penny Coleman, the author of *Flashback: Posttraumatic Stress Disorder, Suicide, and the Lessons of War,* "The names have changed over time, but the phenomenon they describe has remained distressingly constant: war causes mental illness that is life-altering and, in far too may cases, fatal."[14]

> **Soldiers in all wars have experienced PTSD, although prior to 1980 it was called by different names and poorly understood.**

Although PTSD is most commonly associated with combat veterans, the disorder also affects civilians who have experienced trauma. The APA's inclusion of the disorder in the *DSM* was the result of advocacy not only by war veterans but also by the women's movement. By the 1970s feminists had come to realize that rape and child sexual abuse—traumatic events that are more common to women than men—can leave victims with symptoms similar to those experienced by veterans. Therefore, women's groups and veterans both advocated for PTSD's inclusion in the *DSM,* and the definition of the disorder is worded in such a way to include both military and civilian victims of trauma.

The Prevalence of PTSD

The number of people who suffer from PTSD varies among regions and subpopulations. In addition, various studies have arrived at slightly different results because of the methods used to gather and interpret data. According to a large study conducted by the National Institute of Mental Health, 7.8 percent of Americans will suffer from PTSD at some point in their life. To put this number in perspective, it is about the same as the rate of diabetes or coronary heart disease. PTSD strikes about twice as many women as men (10.4 percent versus 5.0 percent, respectively). In any given year, according to the institute, 3.6 percent of Americans will experience PTSD. Again, this number is higher for women (5.2 percent) than for men (1.8 percent).

Diagnosing PTSD

In order to be diagnosed with PTSD, the APA states that the person must have experienced or witnessed an event that involved "actual or threatened death or serious injury, or a threat to the physical integrity of self or others." In addition, the person's response must have "involved intense fear, helplessness, or horror."[15]

In addition, the person must have a certain number of three different types of symptoms—reexperiencing symptoms, avoidance symptoms, and hyperarousal symptoms. Reexperiencing symptoms involve the person reliving the event in some way. The person must have at least one of the following five reexperiencing symptoms: intrusive memories of the event, recurrent dreams of the event, times when the person believes the event is happening again (sometimes called flashbacks), intense psychological distress when exposed to reminders of the event, and intense psychological reactions when exposed to reminders of the event.

Avoidance/numbing symptoms involve the person staying away from things that remind him or her of the event and a general numbing of responses after the event. The person must have at least three of these seven avoidance/numbing symptoms: attempts to avoid thoughts, feelings, or conversations about the event; attempts to avoid activities, places, or people that cause memories of the event; inability to remember an important aspect of the event; reduced interest or participation in significant activities; feeling of detachment or estrangement from others; restricted range of emotions (for example, difficulty having loving feelings); and a sense of a foreshortened future (for example, an inability to imagine having a career, marriage, children, or a normal life span).

Hyperarousal symptoms involve increased anxiety and inability to relax. The person must have at least two of the following five arousal symptoms: difficulty falling or staying asleep; irritability or outbursts of anger; difficulty concentrating; hypervigilance (that is, feeling on edge and alert to feared or imagined threats); and exaggerated startle response (that is, overreacting to external stimuli, such as loud noises).

> " **Hyperarousal symptoms involve increased anxiety and inability to relax.** "

In order to receive a diagnosis of PTSD, the APA states that these symptoms must cause the person "clinically significant distress or impairment in social, occupational, or other important areas of functioning."[16] In addition, the symptoms must have been present for at least four weeks. The prefix *post* in *post-traumatic stress disorder* indicates that the mental illness occurs at a time significantly after the traumatic event. If a person has PTSD-like symptoms during the four weeks following the trauma, they may be diagnosed with a similar disorder known as acute stress disorder (ASD). If these symptoms persist beyond four weeks after the event, the diagnosis is changed from ASD to PTSD.

PTSD Among Young People

Children and teenagers with PTSD have the same symptoms as adults—that is, reexperiencing, avoidance/numbing, and hyperarousal symptoms. In addition, younger children often regress to an earlier stage of their psychological development. For example, young children who no longer suck their thumbs or carry a blanket may return to these behaviors. Because they may have difficulty talking about the traumatic event, they sometimes act it out while playing.

Adolescents with PTSD often become irritable, disrespectful, or disruptive. For example, Gholson J. Lyon, a psychiatrist at the New York University Child Study Center, reported on a 12-year-old boy he referred to as "T" (to protect the boy's confidentiality). T had been both sexually and physically abused as a young child and had been moved among several foster homes. As a result of his difficult youth, T showed symptoms of various mental disorders, including PTSD. "He admitted to getting angry and breaking things and complained of insomnia, nightmares, and frequent nervousness,"[17] Lyon notes. He was also hyperaroused, a state that led him to act out violently toward his peers and adults.

The Impact of PTSD on Sufferers

PTSD takes a heavy toll on its victims and their families. While most people gradually recover from a trauma, others remain trapped in the disturbing events of the past. As Dana Hull writes in the *San Jose Mercury News,* "Some sufferers constantly relive the horror of their experience, with symptoms so severe it's difficult to interact socially, maintain relationships or hang onto a job"[18]

The type of suffering a PTSD patient experiences is often related to the nature of the trauma they have survived. For example, psychologists Victoria Lemle Beckner and John B. Arden describe the case of a person whom they call "Nicole," a victim of child sexual abuse. While Nicole exhibits various symptoms of PTSD into adulthood, perhaps her most distressing problem is her avoidance of intimacy. Because getting close to a partner triggers memories and flashbacks of the sexual abuse inflicted by her uncle, she finds it difficult to develop intimate relationships with men.

In another example, a person whom Beckner and Arden call "Ian" was a victim of a violent robbery. After the attack Ian felt shame for failing to stand up to his attackers. He was also hypervigilant; he installed an expensive burglar alarm in his apartment and had difficulty sleeping. In general, due to his PTSD he found it impossible to feel secure and at peace in his life.

> **While most people gradually recover from a trauma, others remain trapped in the disturbing events of the past.**

War veterans with PTSD essentially continue living the war. They find it impossible to return to civilian life and therefore experience extreme isolation along with their flashbacks, nightmares, and anxiety. Psychologist Daryl S. Paulson describes his experience returning from Vietnam:

Combat memories loomed over me during the day, and the faces of those I had killed haunted me at night. My life became a cycle of suffering—and drinking to relieve the suffering. . . . My life was not just a heap of broken images but a living hell many times worse than anything I had experienced in Vietnam. I was an alcoholic on my 24th birthday and dangerously on the verge of suicide.[19]

Sadly, Paulson's story is similar to those of many other veterans who have struggled to adjust to civilian life while gripped in the throes of PTSD.

Sleep Disturbances and Nightmares

Sleep disturbances and nightmares are among the most troubling symptoms of PTSD. As stated by James Halper, a clinical associate professor of psychiatry at New York University School of Medicine, "These symptoms are considered particularly distressing by patients and have a highly negative impact on their quality of life." In fact, nightmares and sleep disturbances often contribute to substance abuse problems for PTSD suffers, as Halper explains: "Sleep disturbances . . . play a role in substance abuse—especially alcohol—as people attempt to self-medicate to avoid the distress associated with disturbed sleep and/or nightmares."[20] Besides turning to drugs and alcohol, patients also find various ways to avoid sleep, resulting in insomnia.

> **Most people with PTSD (80 percent) have other mental health disorders as well. Many drink or use drugs to ease their anxiety and as a result develop substance abuse problems.**

Mitch Hood, a Marine who served two tours of duty in Iraq, provides a vivid example of the distress caused by nightmares. Hood struggles to keep himself awake all night by chugging energy drinks and popping caffeine tablets. "I'm afraid I'm going to have nightmares and get stuck there," he says. "I try with all my strength not to sleep."[21] When he does sleep, according to *Los Angeles Times* journalist Jia-Rui Chong, "Hood relives combat, or sometimes his mind creates new horror-filled scenarios."[22]

He describes one recurring dream about the day a comrade was killed by a roadside bomb: "I'm up there with my buddy. I pull him out of the humvee. The medevac helicopter is on top of a hill. I'm carrying him. He keeps getting heavier and heavier and sinking into the ground and I drag him. Gravity is increasing. I can't get him to the chopper."[23]

PTSD and Other Disorders

Most people with PTSD (80 percent) have other mental health disorders as well. Many drink or use drugs to ease their anxiety and as a result develop substance abuse problems. Many also suffer from major depression (the most severe form of depression). According to the Institute of Medicine, about half of people with PTSD will have major depression at some point during their lives. Among combat veterans, 98.9 percent of those with PTSD will have some other mental health problem, most likely depression or alcohol use.

In addition to other mental illnesses, war veterans also must often contend with physical disorders, which can contribute to PTSD symptoms. Most notably, many veterans return from combat with traumatic brain injury, wounds to the brain as a result of blows to the head or the concussive effects of nearby explosions. According to the National Institute of Neurological Disorders and Stroke, a division of the National Institutes of Health, symptoms of traumatic brain injury include "headache, confusion, lightheadedness, dizziness, blurred vision or tired eyes, ringing in the ears, . . . a change in sleep patterns, behavioral or mood changes, and trouble with memory, concentration, attention, or thinking."[24] These symptoms are similar to the symptoms of PTSD and can complicate attempts to diagnose and treat veterans for PTSD.

PTSD and Suicide

People with PTSD have a high risk of suicide. The APA reports that people with PTSD are six times as likely as members of the general population to make a first suicide attempt. This rate is twice that of people with other anxiety disorders, although it is only half that of people with mood disorders such as depression or bipolar disorder (manic depression). Young people with PTSD have an increased risk of suicide as well. A study published in the *Archives of General Psychiatry* in March 2009 found that Baltimore youths who had PTSD were five times more likely to attempt suicide than youths who had been exposed to trauma but did not develop PTSD.

The Prognosis for Recovery from PTSD

Of those who develop PTSD, about one-third will have chronic symptoms that will not go away. In some of these people, the experience of trauma can cause long-term personality changes and a diminished quality of life. However, with time and treatment, the remaining two-thirds will recover either partially or completely. Thus, despite the heavy toll PTSD can take on trauma victims and their families, there is hope for the majority of those who suffer from this distressing mental illness. As Laurie B. Slone and Matthew J. Friedman state, "Sixty percent of those who develop PTSD will recover, whether or not they've ever received treatment."[25]

What Is Post-Traumatic Stress Disorder?

66 **For years, people who suffered from PTSD were misunderstood. They were labeled moody, irritable, obnoxious, self-centered, crazy, and sometimes lazy. They did not fit the diagnostic labels of the times, but they were certainly suffering.** 99

—Kendall Johnson, *After the Storm: Healing After Trauma, Tragedy and Terror.* Alameda, CA: Hunter House, 2006.

Johnson is a psychologist who has provided training to Walter Reed Army Medical Center on dealing with stress among returning combat veterans.

66 **Formerly, PTSD was generally considered a condition of male soldiers. However, the feminist movement helped establish that PTSD could also come from other forms of violence—such as domestic abuse or child abuse and rape—that women are more prone to experience.** 99

—Cynthia Piltch and Martha Brown Menard, "Research Shows That Massage Can Be Healing for Your Clients That Suffer from Post-Traumatic Stress Disorder," *Massage Therapy Journal*, Winter 2007.

Piltch teaches at Northeastern University School of Nursing and Tufts Medical School. Menard is the director of research at Potomac Massage Training Institute in Washington, D.C.

* Editor's Note: While the definition of a primary source can be narrowly or broadly defined, for the purposes of Compact Research, a primary source consists of: 1) results of original research presented by an organization or researcher; 2) eyewitness accounts of events, personal experience, or work experience; 3) first-person editorials offering pundits' opinions; 4) government officials presenting political plans and/or policies; 5) representatives of organizations presenting testimony or policy.

> **PTSD is a complex response by humans to protect themselves from a systematic or prolonged threat to their well-being.**

—Daryl S. Paulson and Stanley Krippner, *Haunted by Combat: Understanding PTSD in War Veterans Including Women, Reservists, and Those Coming Back from Iraq.* Westport, CT: Praeger, 2007.

Paulson is a psychologist and veteran who served in Vietnam. Krippner is a professor of psychology at Saybrook Graduate Institute and Research Center.

....

> **In its acute form, PTSD may be like the common cold, experienced at some time in one's life by nearly all.**

—Robert J. Ursano, David M. Benedek, and Carol S. Fullerton, "Posttraumatic Stress Disorder: Neurobiology, Psychology, and Public Health," *Psychiatric Times*, March 2008.

Ursano is the director of the Center for the Study of Traumatic Stress at the Uniformed Services University of the Health Sciences. Benedek is the assistant chair of the center, and Fullerton is the scientific director of the center.

....

> **One cannot talk about *trauma* in general and *Posttraumatic Stress Disorder* (PTSD) specifically without addressing the issue of memory. . . . Posttraumatic Stress Disorder might be viewed as the perpetual memory of fear, danger, or threat.**

—Adam Cash, *Posttraumatic Stress Disorder*. New York: Wiley, 2006.

Cash teaches psychology at the community college and university levels and works as a forensic psychologist with mentally ill criminal offenders.

....

❝Not everyone with PTSD has been through a dangerous event. Some people get PTSD after a friend or family member experiences danger or is harmed.❞

—National Institute of Mental Health, *Post-Traumatic Stress Disorder.* Bethesda, MD: National Institute of Mental Health, 2008. www.nimh.gov.

The National Institute of Mental Health is a division of the U.S. Department of Health and Human Services and is responsible for overseeing research on causes and treatments of mental disorders.

❝Some people may have no or few symptoms of PTSD initially but develop more symptoms over time and others may rapidly develop symptoms that meet the full diagnostic criteria for PTSD.❞

—Institute of Medicine Committee on Gulf War and Health, *Gulf War and Health,* Vol. 6: *Physiologic, Psychologic, and Psychosocial Effects of Deployment-Related Stress.* Washington, DC: National Academies, 2008.

The Institute of Medicine is an independent organization chartered by the U.S. government to conduct research on health-related issues.

❝Re-experiencing symptoms are a sign that your body and mind are actively struggling to cope with the traumatic experience and make sense of what has happened.❞

—Victoria Lemle Beckner and John B. Arden, *Conquering Post-Traumatic Stress Disorder: The Newest Techniques for Overcoming Symptoms, Regaining Hope, and Getting Your Life Back.* Beverly, MA: Far Winds, 2008.

Beckner is a psychology professor at the University of California at San Francisco. Arden is the director of training for mental health at the Kaiser Permanente Medical Centers in northern California.

66 PTSD is more strongly associated with suicide ideation and attempts than any other anxiety disorder. **99**

—Terri Tanielian and Lisa H. Jaycox, eds. *Invisible Wounds of War: Psychological and Cognitive Injuries, Their Consequences, and Services to Assist Recovery.* Santa Monica, CA: Rand, 2008.

Tanielian and Jaycox are codirectors of the Invisible Wounds of War Study Team at the Rand Corporation, a nonprofit public policy research organization in Santa Monica, California.

What Is Post-Traumatic Stress Disorder?

- According to the American Psychiatric Association, between **50 and 60 percent** of people experience some form of trauma during their lifetime.

- At some point in their lifetime, **7.8 percent** of Americans will suffer from PTSD.

- The rate of PTSD is higher among women (**10.4 percent**) than men (**5.0 percent**).

- A nationwide study found that among men, those between the ages of **45 and 54** are at highest risk for PTSD; among women, those between **25 and 34** are at highest risk for PTSD.

- **Women** are more likely than men **to seek treatment** for PTSD.

- Clinicians use **4 different structured interviews** to make a formal diagnosis of PTSD; they contain 17 to 31 questions and take 20 to 60 minutes to complete.

- Among Vietnam veterans with PTSD, **40 percent** had symptoms two decades after returning home from the war.

- Along with their symptoms patients with PTSD also often experience other **consequences of trauma**, including shame, despair, hopelessness, survivor guilt, anger, impulsive and self-destructive behaviors, changed beliefs, and changed personality.

• Two years after the 1995 Oklahoma City bombing, **16 percent** of children in a 100-mile (161km) radius of the blast had symptoms of PTSD.

Women Suffer from PTSD More than Men Do

Some types of trauma affect more men than women, while others affect more women than men. For example, women experience more rape and sexual molestation whereas men experience more physical assaults and accidents. In addition, for reasons that are not completely understood, men and women differ in their likelihood to develop PTSD from any specific traumatic event. For instance, a man who is physically assaulted is much less likely to develop PTSD as a result of the attack than a woman who is assaulted.

Traumatic Event	Prevalence of Event		Prevalence of Lifetime PTSD in Response to Event	
	Men	Women	Men	Women
Rape	0.7%	9.2%	65.0%	45.9%
Molestation	2.8%	12.3%	12.2%	26.5%
Physical assault	11.1%	6.9%	1.8%	21.3%
Accident	25.0%	13.8%	6.3%	8.8%
Natural disaster	18.9%	15.2%	3.7%	5.4%
Witnessed death or injury	40.1%	18.6%	9.1%	2.8%
Learned about a traumatic event	63.1%	61.8%	1.4%	3.2%
Sudden death of a loved one	61.1%	59.0%	12.6%	16.2%

Source: Institute of Medicine Committee on Gulf War and Health, *Gulf War and Health*, Vol. 6: *Physiologic, Psychologic, and Psychosocial Effects of Deployment-Related Stress*. Washington, DC: National Academies, 2008.

The Symptoms of PTSD

In order to be diagnosed with PTSD, a patient must have certain symptoms outlined in the *Diagnostic and Statistical Manual of Mental Disorders*, published by the American Psychiatric Association. The patient must have experienced a traumatic event, at least 1 reexperiencing symptom, 3 avoidance symptoms, and 2 hyperarousal symptoms. In addition, the symptoms must have persisted for more than a month and must be causing significant problems in the patient's life.

A. Exposure to a traumatic event

1. Response involved intense fear, helplessness, or horror

B. Traumatic event is persistently reexperienced in at least one of the following ways:

1. Recurrent and intrusive thoughts or images
2. Recurrent distressing dreams
3. Acting or feeling as if the event were recurring
4. Psychological distress upon exposure to reminders of event
5. Physiological reactions upon exposure to reminders of event

C. Avoidance of stimuli associated with the event and numbing of general response, occurring in at least three of the following ways:

1. Efforts to avoid thoughts, feelings, or conversations about the event
2. Efforts to avoid activities, places, or people that remind person of the event
3. Inability to remember an important aspect of the event
4. Significantly diminished interest or participation in activities
5. Feeling of being detached or estranged from others
6. Restricted range of mood
7. Speaks or thinks of not having a future

D. Increased arousal not present before traumatic event, presenting in at least two of the following ways:

1. Trouble falling or staying asleep
2. Irritability or outburst of anger
3. Difficulty concentrating
4. Hypervigilant (constantly on alert for danger)
5. Exaggerated startle response (on edge)

E. Symptoms last at least one month

F. Symptoms listed above cause significant impairment in daily life

Source: Ben Chavez, "A Review of Pharmacotherapy for PTSD," *U.S. Pharmacist*, November 22, 2006.

Behaviors of Children and Teenagers with PTSD

Children and teenagers with PTSD exhibit the same symptoms as adults, but they may also engage in other distinct behaviors depending on their age. Very young children may unlearn a basic developmental skill, such as speaking or using the toilet. Elementary-school-aged children may develop superstitious beliefs about the event. Preteens are likely to act out the traumatic event while playing. Adolescents may become impulsive and aggressive.

Very young children	Elementary-school-aged children	Adolescents
Generalized fears such as stranger or separation anxiety	Time skew: mis-sequencing trauma-related events when recalling the memory	Post-traumatic re-enactment by in-corporating aspects of the trauma into daily life
Avoidance of situations that may or may not be related to trauma	Omen formation: the belief that there were warning signs that predicted the trauma	Impulsive and aggressive behaviors
Sleep disturbances	References to the trauma in play, drawings or verbalization	
Preoccupation with words or symbols that may or may not be related to the trauma		
Play that repeats themes of the trauma		
Loss of an acquired developmental skill such as toilet training		

Source: Laura J. Greco and Wendy M. Garcia, "Post Traumatic Disorder: Treatment with Confidence, Competence and Compassion," *Access*, July 2008.

Screening for PTSD

Doctors face a formidable challenge when it comes to diagnosing PTSD in their patients. One tool they use is the "Primary Care PTSD Screen," which includes four questions. A patient answering "yes" to any three questions is likely to have PTSD and will often be given a more thorough screening to make a definitive diagnosis.

Primary Care PTSD Screen

Have you ever had any experience that was so frightening, horrible, or upsetting that, in the past month, you:

- Have had nightmares about it or thought about it when you did not want to? **Yes/No**

- Tried hard not to think about it or went out of your way to avoid situations that reminded you of it? **Yes/No**

- Were constantly on guard, watchful, or easily startled? **Yes/No**

- Felt numb or detached from others, activities, or your surroundings? **Yes/No**

Source: Roy Reeves, "Latest Strategies in Diagnosis and Treatment of PTSD," *Medical Economics*, November 21, 2008.

- A study in the *New England Journal of Medicine* found that the rate of PTSD was **6.2 percent** among veterans of the war in Afghanistan and **12 percent** among veterans of the war in Iraq.

- In a study conducted by the National Institute of Mental Health, **88 percent** of men and **79 percent** of women with PTSD had a history of mood, anxiety, or substance-use disorders.

- A study published in the *Clinical Journal of Psychiatry* found that PTSD costs the United States **$3 billion** a year in **lost productivity**.

What Are the Causes of Post-Traumatic Stress Disorder?

> **[PTSD] is . . . one of the very few psychiatric disorders in which the illness is unambiguously caused by a specific external event.**
>
> —David Brody, physician in charge of psychiatric outpatient services at Beth Israel Medical Center in New York City, and Michael Serby, associate chair of the Department of Psychiatry at Beth Israel.

> **As visceral as they may be, traumatic events—explosions, stabbings, car crashes—may be less to blame for PTSD than the brains of the sufferers themselves.**
>
> —Matt Bean, senior editor of *Men's Health* magazine.

Not everyone who experiences a traumatic event develops PTSD. According to the American Psychiatric Association (APA), the nation's largest organization of psychiatrists, 50 to 60 percent of people experience some form of trauma over their lifetime, but a minority (7.8 percent) develop PTSD. Experts are not completely sure why some people get PTSD while others do not. In general, the more stress and trauma a person experiences throughout life, the greater that person's risk of developing PTSD. It may be that these life circumstances are responsible for changes in a person's brain structure and function that leave them vulnerable to developing PTSD when confronted with a major traumatic event.

The Body's Reaction to Stress and Trauma

To discover the causes of PTSD, it is important to understand the human body's natural response to stress. When confronted with a sudden threat, human beings experience many physical and emotional reactions designed to help them cope. The brain releases two types of hormones: adrenalin and cortisol. The adrenaline sets off a "fight-or-flight" response, which helps the person focus on the danger, quickly decide whether to flee or confront it, and act with strength and agility. Physical reactions include accelerated heart and lung functioning, dilated pupils, and tunnel vision. Blood flows away from most vital organs and into the heart and major muscles, providing oxygen that gives the body increased strength. Emotional reactions include fear and anxiety, which motivate the person to act. While adrenaline primes the body to fight or flee, the hormone cortisol prepares it to survive the ongoing danger by raising the level of blood sugar in the body's muscles and brain.

> "When confronted with a traumatic event, the body's stress response can be extreme, affecting how the brain forms memories of the event."

The body's stress response is a normal reaction to danger and is not, in itself, a symptom of PTSD. Anyone who faces danger will experience these physical and emotional changes. When the threat is removed, the brain slows its production of adrenaline and cortisol, and the body and mind return to their prethreat condition.

However, trauma is not a typical threat. When confronted with a traumatic event, the body's stress response can be extreme, affecting how the brain forms memories of the event. Psychiatrists Victoria Lemle Beckner and John B. Arden describe how the stress response, which they call the "stress alarm system," can be overwhelmed in the face of trauma and lead to symptoms of PTSD:

> When you experience a traumatic event . . . adrenaline and cortisol literally flood your brain. This interferes with how your brain normally processes an experience to store it in an organized memory. The trauma memory is fragmented into images, smells, and sounds, and is highly emotional. It is like a live wire in your brain, hot and unpredictable. And anything associated with the trauma

memory—a face, the sound of a helicopter, a dark corridor, the smell of something burning—can set off your alarm system, reactivating it repeatedly and keeping it on constant alert.[26]

Because the trauma memory is so volatile, Beckner and Arden explain, the person with PTSD essentially continues to experience the trauma and all the emotions connected to it in the form of PTSD symptoms, including intrusive memories and nightmares, flashbacks, anxiety, and avoidance and numbing.

Genetics and Brain Functioning

Scientists believe that some people may have a genetic makeup that leaves them vulnerable to PTSD. Specifically, those with the short type of a gene responsible for transporting the brain chemical serotonin are more likely to develop the disorder. Other researchers have focused on genes that make proteins that help the brain create fear memories. Having too much of these proteins may lead to the production of intense, fear-inducing memories and thus to symptoms of PTSD.

Researchers have studied the brains of people with PTSD in an attempt to understand the causes of the disorder. They have found that the structure and activity in certain areas of the brain differ in people with PTSD as compared to people without PTSD. These areas include the amygdala, which is responsible for emotion, learning, and memory, and the prefrontal cortex, which is responsible for controlling the brain's stress response and for extinguishing memories of fearful events. Experts believe that these differences in brain structure and functioning could make people vulnerable to the production of intense, emotion-laden memories that generate the symptoms of PTSD.

Ethnicity and Gender

There is some evidence that certain groups—specifically, blacks, Hispanics, and Native Americans—may be at a greater risk of developing PTSD. Research on combat veterans has found higher rates of PTSD among these groups than among non-Hispanic whites. Experts believe that blacks, Hispanics, and Native Americans may face a higher risk of PTSD because they are more likely to be poor, live in the inner cities, and experience negative life events. In other words, it is their social and economic status rather than their ethnic makeup that puts them at risk.

A person's gender may also contribute to PTSD. Studies consistently find that women are at least twice as likely as men to be diagnosed with the disorder. Some have theorized that this higher rate of PTSD among women reflects the fact that women are more likely than men to experience rape and child sexual abuse. However, recent studies have failed to establish this causal link. As stated by research psychologists David F. Tolin and Edna B. Foa: "The higher prevalence of PTSD among women and girls than among men and boys cannot be attributed solely to a higher risk of adult sexual assault or child sexual abuse."[27] The reason for the disparity in PTSD among women and men remains poorly understood.

> "There is some evidence that certain groups—specifically, blacks, Hispanics, and Native Americans—may be at a greater risk of developing PTSD."

War

Combat veterans and civilians in war zones are at a high risk of PTSD. One study found that 30 percent of Vietnam veterans experienced PTSD at some point following their service, although this number was later adjusted down to 18.7 percent. More recently, another study found that 14 percent of veterans returning from the war in Iraq have the disorder. In addition, refugees from combat zones are also at risk. According to the APA, as many as 70 percent of refugees from Vietnam, Cambodia, and Laos suffer from PTSD. Moreover, people living in war-torn countries face a higher risk of developing the disorder. The rate of PTSD is 37.4 percent in Algeria, 28.4 percent in Cambodia, and 17.8 percent in Gaza.

Child Abuse and Domestic Violence

People who suffer abuse and neglect as children face a higher risk of developing PTSD later in life. As stated by psychiatrist Dragica Kozarić-Kovačić, "Early traumatic experiences (eg, abuse or severe neglect in childhood) may affect the brain structures and functions so as to make a person vulnerable to negative stressful events and more prone to later development of PTSD."[28] One study found that 37.5 percent of child sexual abuse victims, 32.7 percent of physical abuse victims, and 30.6 percent of child neglect victims experienced PTSD. Another study of 31 children who had been sexually abused found that 48 percent had PTSD. As stated by psychologist Stacie E. Putnam, "When children's bodies are used to meet adult needs, there is enormous potential for physical and psychological trauma."[29]

Women who have been victimized by domestic violence are also at greater risk for PTSD. Studies have found that between 45 and 84 percent of battered women had PTSD. Among victims of domestic violence, the greatest risk of developing PTSD is faced by those who have a history of child abuse, who experience chronic violence by multiple partners, who experience violence while pregnant, and who experience more severe forms of violence, such as rape.

Terrorism and Natural Disasters

Rates of PTSD tend to rise in the wake of terrorist attacks and natural disasters. For example, a study of survivors of the 1995 Oklahoma City bombing found 34.3 percent had PTSD. More recently, researchers found that 7.5 percent of New Yorkers and 20 percent of residents of lower Manhattan developed PTSD following the terrorist attacks of September 11, 2001. A follow-up study published in the *American Journal of Epidemiology* 6 months after the attack found that the rate of PTSD had returned to its typical preattack level. Another study focused on those directly exposed to the attack found higher and more persistent rates of PTSD. Among rescue and recovery workers, office workers, residents, and people passing by at the time of the event, 14.1 percent had PTSD 2 to 3 years after the attack, and 19.1 percent had PTSD 5 to 6 years after the attack, according to the August 2009 report published in the *Journal of the American Medical Association*. The researchers attributed the increase to the cumulative stress of repercussions of the event, such as the loss of a job or loved one.

> " Studies have found that between 45 and 84 percent of battered women had PTSD. "

Natural disasters also result in high rates of PTSD. Hurricane Katrina, which roared through the American Gulf Coast in August 2005, provides a sad example. The storm caused more than $100 billion in damage, left more than 1,800 people dead, and over a million homeless. A landmass the size of the United Kingdom—90,000 square miles (233,099 sq. km)—was declared a disaster area. The psychological toll was equally dramatic: One study found that 30 percent of people from New Orleans and 12 percent of people from the surrounding hurricane-afflicted region suffered from PTSD 5 months after the storm. Another study compared the rates of PTSD 5 to 7 months after Katrina and again 1 year after that. This study found that 5 to 7 months after the disaster, the rate of PTSD was 26 percent in New Orleans and 12 percent in the surrounding area; 1 year later the rate of PTSD was 24 percent in New Orleans and 20 percent in the surrounding area. Thus, the rate had decreased slightly in New Orleans (although it still remained high) but had actually increased in the surrounding area.

> "Resilience factors include the willingness to seek help from family and friends, a strong social support system, good coping skills, and a positive, optimistic outlook."

Resilience as a Preventive Factor

Experts suggest that many people possess resilience factors that make them able to endure trauma and recover without experiencing persistent PTSD symptoms. Resilience factors include the willingness to seek help from family and friends, a strong social support system, good coping skills, and a positive, optimistic outlook. In short a person who is happy and psychologically stable at the time of the traumatic event is less likely to develop PTSD than a person who has been through many negative life events, has little social support, and may be suffering from a preexisting mental illness such as depression.

Recent research suggests that children may be more resilient in the face of trauma than adults. One researcher at Duke University Medical Center studied 1,420 children over the course of several years. He found that 68 percent of the young people experienced trauma. Of those who were exposed to trauma, 13.4 percent developed at least 1 symptom, and those who had experienced more than 1 trauma or had been exposed to sexual or violent events developed more symptoms. However, only 0.5 percent of the young people met the criteria for a diagnosis of PTSD, a rate much lower than that found in studies of adults.

Secondary PTSD

Trauma victims are not the only people who experience symptoms of PTSD. Health-care professionals who treat trauma victims are also vulnerable to the disorder. One study found that 15 percent of social workers experience PTSD at some point in life, a rate nearly double that of the general population. In addition to mental health workers, the family members of trauma victims, such as the wives and children of returning combat veterans, can also be affected. This phenomenon is known as secondary PTSD, vicarious traumatization, or compassion fatigue.

A Complex Disorder

No one knows why two people who experience the same event can have different reactions—with one developing PTSD and the other bouncing back to a normal level of functioning. Most researchers believe there is no single answer. Rather, susceptibility to PTSD is dependent on each person's individual family background, history of mental illness or child abuse, genetic makeup, brain structure and functioning, and the nature, severity, and duration of the trauma he or she experiences. On the other hand, a person's ability to ward off the disorder depends on resilience factors such as social supports and a positive worldview. Thus, while traumatic events may seem random, unpredictable, and seemingly without meaning, the mystery of PTSD appears to be increasingly within the grasp of human understanding.

What Are the Causes of
Post-Traumatic Stress Disorder?

66 **When you're suffering from PTSD, the short answer to what's going on inside your head and body is that your healthy stress system has been strained by trauma.** 99

—Victoria Lemle Beckner and John B. Arden, *Conquering Post-Traumatic Stress Disorder: The Newest Techniques for Overcoming Symptoms, Regaining Hope, and Getting Your Life Back.* Beverly, MA: Far Winds, 2008.

Beckner is a psychology professor at the University of California at San Francisco. Arden is the director of training for mental health at the Kaiser Permanente Medical Centers in northern California.

66 **Not everyone who has been through a traumatic event suffers from PTSD. . . . It's normal to lose sleep, and replay the scene over and over in the head in the days and weeks after an event. Most people soon let these feelings go.** 99

—Stew Magnuson, "Combat Stress: To Heal Psychological Trauma, Troops Relive War in Virtual Reality," *National Defense*, December 2008.

Magnuson is a Washington, D.C.–based journalist who serves as senior editor of *National Defense* magazine.

* Editor's Note: While the definition of a primary source can be narrowly or broadly defined, for the purposes of Compact Research, a primary source consists of: 1) results of original research presented by an organization or researcher; 2) eyewitness accounts of events, personal experience, or work experience; 3) first-person editorials offering pundits' opinions; 4) government officials presenting political plans and/or policies; 5) representatives of organizations presenting testimony or policy.

❝It is the inability to forget the trauma that leads to pathology and suffering in PTSD.❞

—Robert J. Ursano, David M. Benedek, and Carol S. Fullerton, "Posttraumatic Stress Disorder: Neurobiology, Psychology, and Public Health," *Psychiatric Times*, March 2008.

Ursano is the director of the Center for the Study of Traumatic Stress at the Uniformed Services University of the Health Sciences. Benedek is the assistant chair of the center, and Fullerton is the scientific director of the center.

....

❝Memories of overwhelming and threatening events are stored differently than normal memories. The emotions and bodily sensations of the moment are linked with the visual memory in such a way that the memory becomes too powerful for the mind to integrate.❞

—Kendall Johnson, *After the Storm: Healing After Trauma, Tragedy and Terror.* Alameda, CA: Hunter House, 2006.

Johnson is a psychologist who has provided training to Walter Reed Army Medical Center on dealing with stress among returning combat veterans.

....

❝Unlike psychic or physical wounds . . . traumas responsible for PTSD remain a source of distress. This means that the original trauma, rather than being relegated to the past, is still a powerful influence on a person's behavior.❞

—Daryl S. Paulson and Stanley Krippner, *Haunted by Combat: Understanding PTSD in War Veterans Including Women, Reservists, and Those Coming Back from Iraq.* Westport, CT: Praeger, 2007.

Paulson is a psychologist and a veteran of the U.S. Marines who served in Vietnam. Krippner is a professor of psychology at Saybrook Graduate Institute and Research Center.

....

66 Research has documented stress reactions . . . in youth exposed to disasters. . . . PTSD appears to be the most prevalent post-disaster disorder. **99**

—Betty Pfefferbaum et al., "Youth's Reactions to Disasters and the Factors That Influence Their Response," *Prevention Researcher*, September 2008.

Pfefferbaum is the chair of the Department of Psychiatry and Behavioral Sciences at the University of Oklahoma Health Sciences Center.

66 Three factors influencing the likelihood that a child or adolescent will develop [PTSD] are severity of the traumatic event, parental reaction to the traumatic event and physical proximity to the traumatic event. **99**

—Laura J. Greco and Wendy M. Garcia, "Post Traumatic Stress Disorder: Treatment with Confidence, Competence and Compassion," *Access*, July 2008.

Greco and Garcia are both assistant professors at the Fones School of Dental Hygiene at the University of Bridgeport in Connecticut.

66 Personality and cognitive factors, such as optimism and the tendency to view challenges in a positive or negative way, as well as social factors, such as the availability and use of social support, appear to influence how people adjust to trauma. **99**

—National Institute of Mental Health, "NIMH Fact Sheet: Post-Traumatic Stress Disorder Research," 2007. www.nimh.gov.

The National Institute of Mental Health is an agency of the U.S. government that sponsors research on the causes and treatments of mental disorders.

Facts and Illustrations

What Are the Causes of Post-Traumatic Stress Disorder?

- **Rape** and **physical assault** are the most common causes of PTSD among American women; **military combat** is the most common cause of PTSD among men.

- A study published in the *Journal of the American Academy of Child and Adolescent Psychiatry* found that of 31 children who had been sexually abused, **48 percent** had PTSD.

- According to the American Psychiatric Association, a study of Vietnam veterans found that **21 percent** of black soldiers experienced PTSD while **14 percent** of whites developed the disorder.

- A study published in the *Journal of the American Medical Association* found that **20 percent** of the residents of Manhattan had PTSD 5 to 8 weeks after the September 11, 2001, attacks that destroyed the Twin Towers of the World Trade Center and killed over **2,600 people**.

- According to a study conducted by the Royal College of Psychiatry, after a July 2005 suicide bombing in London that killed 56 people and injured about 700, **30 to 40 percent** of victims developed PTSD, and **20 percent** had symptoms 2 years after the attack.

- A study conducted by the UCLA/Duke University National Center for Child Traumatic Stress found that **9.7 percent** of students directly exposed to a school shooting in Santee, California, had PTSD 8 to 9 months after the shooting.

PTSD and the Brain

Researchers have found that the size and functioning of several parts of the brain differ in people with PTSD as compared to those without PTSD. Three of these areas include the amygdala and two regions of the prefrontal cortex (PFC): the medial PFC and the ventromedial PFC. The amygdala controls memory, emotion, and learning. The medial PFC regulates the brain's stress response. The ventromedial PFC helps the brain extinguish fearful memories. Poor functioning of these three areas of the brain could be responsible for the distorted, emotion-charged memories that cause the distressing symptoms experienced by those with PTSD.

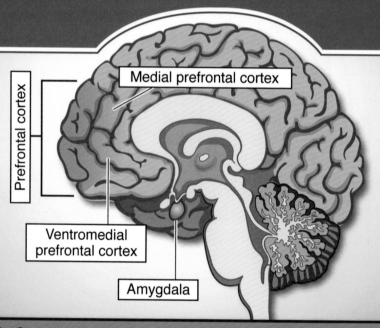

Brain Structures Involved in Dealing with Fear and Stress

Source: National Institute of Mental Health, "NIMH: Fact Sheet: Post-Traumatic Stress Disorder Research," 2007. www.nimh.gov.

- A 2009 study published in *Biomed Central Psychiatry* found that **67 percent** of people abducted by Ugandan rebels and forced to serve in the military developed PTSD.

- A study published in the *Pakistan Journal of Medical Sciences* found that of 210 victims of an October 2005 earthquake in Pakistan, 119 (**57 percent**) developed PTSD; of those who sustained physical injuries, **62 percent** developed PTSD.

Rate of PTSD Among People Exposed to the September 11, 2001, Attack on New York City

One study found a high rate of PTSD among people directly exposed to the September 11, 2001, attack in New York City that destroyed the Twin Towers of the World Trade Center and killed over 2,600 people. The study included rescue and recovery workers, office workers, residents in the area, and people who were passing by at the time of the attack. The rate was high 2 to 3 years after the attack and went up even higher 5 to 6 years after the attack. Researchers believe that the rise in cases was due to repercussions of the original event, such as job losses or health problems, which caused increased stress over time.

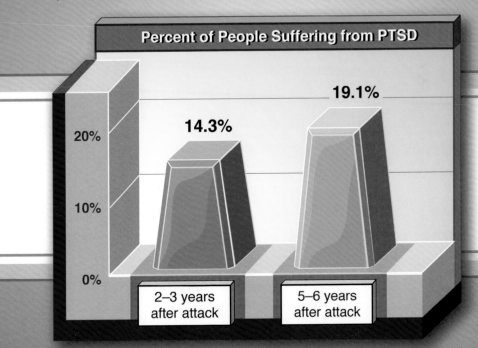

Percent of People Suffering from PTSD

14.3% — 2–3 years after attack

19.1% — 5–6 years after attack

Source: Robert M. Brackbill et al., "Asthma and Posttraumatic Stress Symptoms 5 to 6 Years Following Exposure to the World Trade Center Terrorist Attack," *JAMA*, August 5, 2009.

Rates of PTSD Following Hurricane Katrina

The rates of PTSD were high following Hurricane Katrina. Seventeen to 20 months after the disaster, the rate of PTSD had fallen slightly in New Orleans, although it still remained high. Moreover, the rate had increased significantly in the remainder of the Gulf region. Researchers believe the continuing high rates of PTSD are the result of the slow pace of recovery in the region, especially in rural areas, where mental health treatment and other services are less readily available.

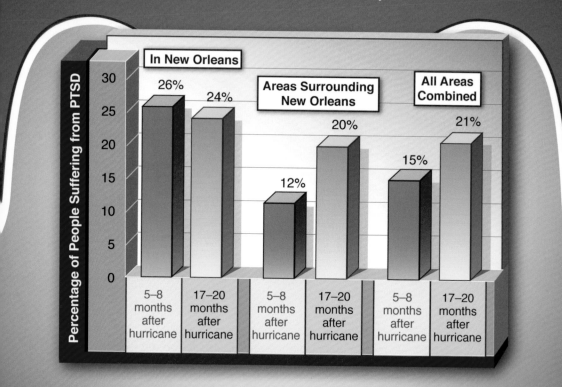

Source: Ronald C. Kessler et al., "Trends in Mental Illness and Suicidality After Hurricane Katrina," *Molecular Psychiatry*, vol. 13, 2008.

- A study published in the June 2009 issue of *Clinical Practice and Epidemiological Studies in Mental Health* found that 3 months after a tsunami struck Thailand in 2004, the rate of PTSD was **33.6 percent**; 6 months after the tsunami, the rate of PTSD was **21.6 percent**.

- A study published in the *British Medical Journal* found that **one-third** of children in automobile accidents developed symptoms of PTSD.

- A 2007 paper published by the American Psychological Association states that **25 to 33 percent** of Americans involved in automobile accidents develop PTSD.

- A study of 900 U.S. mothers conducted by Harris Interactive for Childbirth Connection found that **9 percent** developed PTSD as a result of childbirth.

- Researchers with the Women's Stress Disorder Treatment Team in the Albuquerque-based New Mexico Veterans Affairs Health Care System estimate that **80 to 90 percent** of female veterans with PTSD are victims of sexual trauma.

How Can Post-Traumatic Stress Disorder Be Treated?

> ❝ A significant percentage of patients may remain symptomatic for many years, and PTSD can, even with treatment, become permanently disabling. ❞

—David Brody, physician in charge of psychiatric outpatient services at Beth Israel Medical Center in New York City, and Michael Serby, associate chair in the Department of Psychiatry at Beth Israel.

> ❝ PTSD does not have to become chronic and debilitating. If promptly diagnosed, it can often be successfully treated in weeks or months, not years. ❞

—Richard Ransley, clinical supervisor of the Santa Fe Rape Crisis and Trauma Treatment Center in New Mexico.

Mr. A, whose name has been withheld to protect his privacy, was working in the World Trade Center on September 11, 2001, the day terrorists attacked and brought down the Twin Towers, killing more than 2,600 people. Although he escaped the building alive, months later he continued to suffer emotional scars. As described by psychiatrists David Brody and Michael Serby, "Mr. A was unable to sleep more than a few hours at a stretch. He was tense and anxious. . . . Mr. A. became withdrawn, depressed, and detached. Recollections of what he had witnessed—his coworkers' panic, the doomed firemen rushing by him in the stairwell, the falling bodies—intruded into his thoughts."[30]

Mr. A was clearly suffering from PTSD. Fortunately, at the urging of his family, he eventually sought help. He was prescribed an antidepressant medication and began attending psychotherapy sessions. Soon his sleep improved, he felt less depressed, and he began making plans to attend school and begin a new career. Although he continued to feel anxious when reminded of the attack, he was able to move on with his life and get a new job and a steady girlfriend.

As Mr. A's story illustrates, the main treatments for PTSD are psychotherapy and medication. Brody and Serby explain, "The treatment of PTSD is two-pronged: medication to blunt the more disabling anxiety symptoms and psychotherapy to restore normal stress responses."[31] Therapy and medication are often used in combination but are also used separately.

Types of Psychotherapy for PTSD

Various kinds of psychotherapy are used in the treatment of PTSD. Most of them fall under the umbrella of a type of therapy known as cognitive-behavioral therapy, sometimes known as trauma-focused cognitive-behavioral therapy. Broadly defined, this form of therapy involves helping the patient change his or her thoughts (cognitions) in response to triggers or hot spots that bring on PTSD symptoms. There are several different types of cognitive-behavioral therapy, including exposure therapy, cognitive-processing therapy, and eye movement desensitization and reprocessing.

In exposure therapy, sometimes called prolonged-exposure therapy, the person with PTSD essentially reexperiences the traumatic event in the safety of the therapist's office. Through the use of mental imagery, talking, or writing, the patient repeatedly relives the event with increasing degrees of exposure. In this way the patient comes to view the event objectively rather than being overwhelmed by fear with each memory, and his or her PTSD symptoms diminish. As described by Laurie B. Slone and Matthew J. Friedman, "The goal of treatment is to disconnect the memory from the intolerable sense of fear and stress with which it has been associated."[32]

Often used in conjunction with exposure therapy, cognitive processing therapy employs a technique known as cognitive restructuring. The patient and therapist identify negative or counterproductive thoughts related to the traumatic event and systematically change them. In this way the patient can retrain the way he or she thinks about the event and the triggers that bring back the traumatic feelings, decreasing the event's power to induce fear, helplessness, guilt, and shame. As described by the Institute of Medicine, cognitive-processing therapy "targets negative *beliefs* by confronting distorted traumatic memories, and attempts are made to change or modify the erroneous beliefs and subsequently inappropriate responses."[33]

> ❝ Therapy and medication are often used in combination but are also used separately. ❞

In eye movement desensitization and reprocessing, another form of therapy, the power of the patient's traumatic memories is decreased through the use of rapid eye movement. While thinking about the traumatic event, the patient watches the therapist move his or her finger back and forth quickly and makes positive statements. The theory behind this therapy is that PTSD symptoms result because the brain does not completely process information related to a traumatic event; therefore, negative perceptions, disturbing emotions, and distorted thoughts are stored in the mind as they were originally experienced during the trauma. For reasons that are not completely understood, eye movement desensitization and reprocessing is thought to allow patients to complete the processing of the information in a way that will permit rational thoughts, realistic perceptions, and less upsetting emotions to be associated with the event.

Virtual Reality

In recent years some therapists have been using virtual reality as part of the exposure therapy process. In virtual reality the patient wears a headset that presents an audio and visual simulation of his or her traumatic event. So far, programs have been developed for terrorist attacks and combat situations. While the effectiveness of virtual reality has not yet been proved in scientific studies, experts are enthusiastic about its potential to reexpose patients to their trauma in a safe way, helping them confront their feelings of fear and helplessness and ultimately experience a decrease in their stress-related anxiety and other PTSD symptoms. As stated by *Newsweek* reporter Christopher Werth, "By establishing a context for patients to tell their stories, it can help kick-start the therapeutic process."[34]

Medications for PTSD

Doctors use many different medications to treat PTSD. They most commonly prescribe a type of drug known as a selective serotonin reuptake inhibitor. These drugs are believed to work by regulating the level of the brain chemical serotonin. Although they are antidepressants, meaning they are usually given to people with depression, they are also prescribed to patients with PTSD to help them with symptoms such as anxiety, excessive worrying, sadness, and feeling numb inside. Doctors also prescribe other, older types of antidepressants, including drugs called tricyclic antidepressants and monoamine oxidase inhibitors.

Besides antidepressants, doctors also prescribe drugs known as benzodiazepines to people with PTSD. These drugs are used to treat anxiety, insomnia, and irritability—all of which are PTSD symptoms. Other drugs are used more rarely. They include mood stabilizers and antipsychotic drugs, which are more commonly given to people with bipolar disorder (also known as manic depression) and schizophrenia. Anticonvulsants, which are normally used to control seizures in people with epilepsy, prevent migraines, and treat various brain disorders, are also sometimes prescribed to people with PTSD.

> " In eye movement desensitization and reprocessing, . . . the power of the patient's traumatic memories is decreased through the use of rapid eye movement. "

Therapy, Drugs, or Both?

The decision about whether to use therapy, drugs, or both is usually made by the patient and doctor working together. Some people do not like the idea of therapy, and their symptoms may be eased by medication. Others oppose medication on principle or are unwilling to tolerate the side effects; for them, therapy might be a better option. As Slone and Friedman state, "If you want to talk about your trauma and don't want to take medication, you'd be a candidate for psychotherapy. On the other hand, if you don't want to discuss your traumatic experiences, you'd be a likely candidate for medication."[35]

Donna B., whose last name was withheld to protect her privacy, is a typical example of a PTSD patient treated with both psychotherapy and medication. Suffering from PTSD as a result of a rape at the age of 16 followed by two abusive marriages, Donna eventually sought treatment and received both medication and cognitive behavioral therapy, which helped her cope with her illness and go on to volunteer at a domestic abuse organization. Describing her process of recovering, she states: "My PTSD is triggered a lot by [my ex-husband], yet I'm trying to take ownership and control *it* instead of the PTSD controlling me."[36]

Treating Children and Teens with PTSD

Sadly, young people are often among the victims of trauma. Psychotherapy is generally the treatment of choice for young patients. However, young children have difficulty expressing their thoughts and feelings with words. For that reason, therapists will usually use play therapy with children under the age of nine. As explained by psychologist Gayle Zieman, "Play therapy allows children . . . to act out their fears with toys and people figures."[37] This process permits them to relive and communicate about the trauma and thereby ease the fear connected to the memories of the event.

> " The decision about whether to use therapy, drugs, or both is usually made by the patient and doctor working together. "

With older children and teens, PTSD treatments are generally the same as for adults. With older youths, however, medications are less commonly used, and family therapy may be included. Family therapy involves the whole family in the therapy sessions rather than just the child or teen. As Zieman explains, "Children often feel very supported when parents and siblings attend therapy with them and work as a group."[38]

The story of Kareem helps to illustrate how a combination of therapies can help a teenager with PTSD. Kareem is a 13-year-old British boy who was involved in a car accident in which a man was seriously injured. Months after the crash, he had bad dreams and intrusive memories of the event. He began sleeping with his parents, which he had not done for years, and avoiding cars and streets. Eventually, his parents took him to see a therapist, Clare, who helped him with both family therapy and exposure therapy.

Kareem says: "I've seen Clare 6 times now, I go every week. Sometimes Mum and Dad come too. We talk and also do stuff outside, practical stuff

Clare says will help me to be less frightened about cars and roads. I do get scared when we go out of her office and onto the pavement, but she talks me through it and we stay outside until I feel ok again."[39] Kareem's description provides an excellent example of exposure therapy at work.

By exposing Kareem to the situations that bring back his disturbing memories, Clare helped him to overcome his fears, and his PTSD symptoms gradually lessened.

Preventing PTSD

Experts believe it is possible to prevent PTSD. For example, some contend that people with jobs that expose them to traumatic events—such as soldiers, paramedics, nurses, and disaster relief workers—can be trained in what to expect on the job and in the use of coping skills to reduce the effects of disturbing experiences. These coping skills include seeking support and talking about their experiences as a way of defusing the memories and triggers that lead to PTSD symptoms.

In addition to training workers, researchers believe that intervening quickly after a traumatic event such as a natural disaster or terrorist attack can help prevent the emergence of PTSD symptoms later.

> " In some cases trauma can lead to personal growth as victims search for meaning from their experience and forge a new awareness of life and their place in the world. "

This approach, sometimes referred to as psychological first aid or psychological debriefing, is believed to help the trauma victim to make sense of what has happened, feel less alone, and begin the process of healing. However, there is conflicting evidence about the effectiveness of this approach. Studies have suggested that a single session of psychological debriefing can actually do more harm than good by essentially stirring up feelings without providing the follow-up treatment that is needed for a full recovery. Some experts recommend a more targeted approach in which only those at risk for PTSD are given treatment after a trauma.

Some researchers believe that PTSD can be prevented with a medication known as a beta-blocker. This drug is believed to make the memories of traumatic experiences less emotional by suppressing the production of hormones in the trauma victim. Some researchers are excited by the prospect of using such drugs to prevent the development of PTSD symptoms in trauma sufferers, including combat veterans and victims of natural disasters or terrorist attacks. However, others are concerned about the ethical implications of fiddling with people's memories of horrific events, likening it to "playing God."

Post-Traumatic Growth

PTSD is a severe, debilitating mental illness with often tragic consequences for individuals and their families. However, with time and treatment, people with PTSD are often able to heal their psychic wounds and move on with their lives. In some cases trauma can lead to personal growth as victims search for meaning from their experience and forge a new awareness of life and their place in the world. As stated by Victoria Lemle Beckner and John B. Arden: "Many people have found that their traumas helped them grow into wiser, stronger, and more compassionate human beings. This growth enabled them to give back to others—to contribute to their families and communities in new ways, and make a difference in others' lives."[40] For some, then, the suffering of PTSD has the unintended consequence of a renewed sense of purpose and engagement with the world.

How Can Post-Traumatic Stress Disorder Be Treated?

66 Traumatic events such as the Sept. 11 attacks, Hurricane Katrina, and the wars in Iraq and Afghanistan have enabled researchers to learn a lot more about how best to treat post-traumatic stress disorder. 99

—Tori DeAngelis, "PTSD Treatments Grow in Evidence, Effectiveness," *Monitor on Psychology*, January 2008, www.apa.org.

DeAngelis is a writer who has worked for *Psychology Today* and the American Psychological Association's *Monitor on Psychology*.

66 Treatment of PTSD has not received the level of research activity needed to support conclusions about the potential benefits of treatment modalities. 99

—Institute of Medicine Committee on Treatment of Posttraumatic Stress Disorder, *Treatment of Posttraumatic Stress Disorder: An Assessment of the Evidence*. Washington, DC: National Academies, 2008.

The Institute of Medicine is an independent organization chartered by the U.S. government to conduct research into medical issues.

* Editor's Note: While the definition of a primary source can be narrowly or broadly defined, for the purposes of Compact Research, a primary source consists of: 1) results of original research presented by an organization or researcher; 2) eyewitness accounts of events, personal experience, or work experience; 3) first-person editorials offering pundits' opinions; 4) government officials presenting political plans and/or policies; 5) representatives of organizations presenting testimony or policy.

❝Exposure therapy appears to be one of the most routinely examined and empirically supported treatments for PTSD.❞

—Christina M. Hassija and Matt J. Gray, "Behavioral Interventions for Trauma and Posttraumatic Stress Disorder," *International Journal of Behavioral Consultation and Therapy*, 2007.

Hassija is a graduate student in clinical psychology at the University of Wyoming. Gray is an associate professor of clinical psychology at the University of Wyoming.

❝I cannot express to you the enormous relief I felt when I discovered my condition was real and treatable. . . . I began taking medication, which in combination with behavioral therapy, marked the turning point in my regaining control of my life.❞

—P.K. Philips, "My Story of Survival: Battling PTSD," Anxiety Disorders Association of America, 2009. www.adaa.org.

Philips was diagnosed at age 35 with PTSD resulting from a history of child abuse and rape.

❝Not until I sought professional help did I realize that talking about it was the best cure. I still have trouble today dealing with it, and I still take medication prescribed to me by a doctor.❞

—Anonymous, "A Letter to My Brothers from an Anonymous Marine," *Exceptional Parent*, May 2008.

The author is a U.S. Marine who served in combat and developed PTSD.

66 I have treated hundreds of PTSD patients using EMDR [eye movement desensitization and reprocessing], and the vast majority of them improved completely. 99

—Robert P. Salvatore, "Posttraumatic Stress Disorder: A Treatable Public Health Problem," *Health and Social Work*, May 2009.

Salvatore is a licensed clinical social worker in Nashua, New Hampshire.

66 PTSD is a complex and multidimensional latticework of symptoms, memories, events, responses, and beliefs, and treatment hinges on these complex intersections. 99

—Jeffrey Kirkwood, "Private Traumas, Personal Mythologies: Post-Traumatic Stress Disorder Among Combat Veterans," introduction to *Haunted by Combat: Understanding PTSD in War Veterans Including Women, Reservists, and Those Coming Back from Iraq*, by Daryl S. Paulson and Stanley Krippner. Westport, CT: Praeger, 2007.

Kirkwood has a master's degree in philosophy from the University of Chicago. He has done research on international human rights and psychology.

66 PTSD will be the first mental disorder to be preventable. It already is. 99

—Robert J. Ursano, David M. Benedek, and Carol S. Fullerton, "Posttraumatic Stress Disorder: Neurobiology, Psychology, and Public Health," *Psychiatric Times*, March 2008.

Ursano is director of the Center for the Study of Traumatic Stress at the Uniformed Services University of the Health Sciences. Benedek is the assistant chair of the center, and Fullerton is the scientific director of the center.

"Erasing the pain of difficult memories [with beta-blockers] sounds like a dream come true. . . . But the idea also raises concerns. Such memories, after all, are an integral part of a person."

—Emily Singer, "Manipulating Memory," *Technology Review*, May/June 2009.

Singer is the senior editor for biomedicine at *Technology Review* magazine.

"Tragedy and pain cannot be avoided in our ordinary lives, but they can take on new meaning as they are integrated into a broader healing framework."

—Richard F. Mollica, *Healing Invisible Wounds: Paths to Hope and Recovery in a Violent World.* Orlando, FL: Harcourt, 2006.

Mollica is a psychiatry professor at Harvard Medical School and the director of the Harvard Program in Refugee Trauma.

"There are five main areas of personal growth that people talk about after traumatic events. . . . They are spiritual growth, improved sense of self, enhanced relationships, a general appreciation of the value of life and being set on a positive new life course or new life path."

—Joshua Norman, "Traumas Can Lead to Spiritual Growth," *Biloxi (MS) Sun Herald*, December 23, 2007.

Norman is a health reporter for the *Biloxi (MS) Sun Herald*. In 2007 he studied mental health issues in the wake of Hurricane Katrina as a media fellow with the Henry J. Kaiser Family Foundation.

Facts and Illustrations

How Can Post-Traumatic Stress Disorder Be Treated?

- **Psychotherapy** for PTSD typically lasts three to six months. It may last up to a year if the patient has other disorders along with PTSD.

- Most people who take **antidepressant medication** for PTSD improve within nine months, but they typically continue taking the medication even after symptoms improve.

- A study conducted at the Center for Traumatic Stress at Hadassah University Hospital in Jerusalem found that trauma patients treated with cognitive-behavioral therapy and exposure therapy developed PTSD at rates of **18 percent** and **21 percent**, respectively. Patients treated with an antidepressant developed the disorder at a rate of 61 percent.

- One study of survivors of Hurricane Katrina found that only **32 percent** of those who had a mental disorder such as PTSD received treatment.

- The only two drugs approved by the Food and Drug Administration for the treatment of PTSD are the antidepressants **sertraline** (Zoloft) and **paroxetine** (Paxil); however, doctors prescribe many other drugs as well.

- Many of the drugs prescribed for PTSD have **side effects**, including headaches, nausea, agitation, and suicidal thoughts and behaviors.

Types of Therapy for PTSD

Various types of therapy are used in the treatment of PTSD, and many of them overlap. Shown here is a partial list of therapies and their components.

Cognitive-Behavioral Therapy (CBT), also known as Trauma-Focused Cognitive-Behavioral Therapy (TFCBT)	A broad category of therapy in which the goal is to change the thought process in order to change thoughts, feelings, and behaviors related to the traumatic event.
Exposure Therapy, also known as Prolonged Exposure Therapy	A type of CBT in which the patient talks about the trauma event repeatedly and with increasing detail in order to lessen the memories' power to induce fear and produce PTSD symptoms.
Cognitive Processing Therapy	A type of CBT in which the patient creates a written narrative of the traumatic event and uses a technique called cognitive re-structuring to replace erroneous, upsetting thoughts with more balanced, realistic ones.
Eye Movement Desensitization and Reprocessing (EMDR)	A type of CBT in which the patient moves his or her eyes back and forth while thinking of the traumatic event in order to lessen the power of the trauma memories.
Stress Inoculation Training	A type of CBT in which the patient does not discuss the trauma but instead focuses on stopping the thoughts that cause anxiety and other PTSD symptoms.
Psychodynamic Therapy	Therapy in which the patient and therapist work together to uncover suppressed thoughts and feelings related to the trauma in order to gain mastery of them.
Group Therapy	Therapy in which several people with PTSD meet to discuss their experiences and share ways to cope with their symptoms.
Marriage and Family Therapy	Therapy in which couples or families meet as a group to improve communication, resolve conflicts, and provide support to the PTSD patient.
Psychoeducation	Therapy in which the patient learns about PTSD and its symptoms.
Peer Counseling	Therapy in which the patient meets with another PTSD sufferer rather than with a therapist.

Medications Used for PTSD

Various types of drugs are used for the treatment of PTSD. Shown here is a partial list of the kinds of drugs and their role in treating PTSD symptoms.

Selective Serotonin Reuptake Inhibitors (SSRIs)	A newer type of antidepressant that is also used for anxiety. Most treatment guidelines list SSRIs as the first choice in drug treatment for PTSD.
Tricyclic Antidepressants (TCAs)	An older type of antidepressant, named for its three-pronged molecular structure. Due to their side effects, they are usually a second-choice treatment behind SSRIs for PTSD.
Monoamine Oxidase Inhibitors (MAOIs)	An older type of antidepressant, named for its suppression of any enzyme in the brain that is thought to control mood. Due to their side effects, they are usually a second-choice treatment behind SSRIs for PTSD.
Alpha-Adrenergic Blockers	A hypertension drug that is used to reduce nightmares, improve sleep, and ease other symptoms in patients with PTSD.
Anticonvulsants	Typically used to treat seizures in people with epilepsy and mood instability in people with bipolar disorder (manic depression), they are rarely used for PTSD.
Atypical Antipsychotics	A newer type of antipsychotic typically used for people with schizophrenia and bipolar disorder (manic depression). They are used for people with PTSD who do not respond to other drugs or who have psychotic symptoms (delusions or hallucinations).
Benzodiazepines	Antianxiety drugs that are used to treat anxiety, insomnia, and irritability. They are generally not recommended for PTSD because they are highly addictive and there is little evidence that they are effective for PTSD symptoms.
Beta-Blockers	Drugs that are thought to block brain hormones and lessen the fear associated with traumatic memories, thereby preventing symptoms of PTSD.

Sources: Ben Chavez: "A Review of Pharmacotherapy for PTSD," *U.S. Pharmacist*, November 22, 2006; Institute of Medicine Committee on Treatment of Posttraumatic Stress Disorder, *Treatment of Posttraumatic Stress Disorder: An Assessment of the Evidence*. Washington, DC: National Academies, 2008.

Mental Distraction May Help Alleviate PTSD Flashbacks

Researchers at Oxford University predicted that they could prevent flashbacks—a primary symptom of PTSD—by interfering with the brain's ability to form mental images in the immediate aftermath of trauma. They tested their theory by showing a traumatic film depicting injury and death, then asking viewers to either play the video game Tetris or do nothing for 10 minutes. They found that the participants who played Tetris had significantly fewer flashbacks during the following week. From these results, the researchers concluded that it may be possible to prevent PTSD flashbacks by impeding the brain's ability to form distressing visual memories.

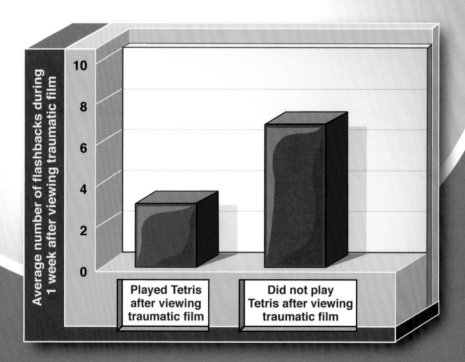

Source: Emily A. Holmes et al., "Can Playing the Computer Game 'Tetris' Reduce the Build-Up of Flashbacks for Trauma? A Proposal from Cognitive Science," *PLoS ONE*, vol. 4, no. 1, 2009. www.plosone.org.

- A study approved by the Food and Drug Administration found that the **hallucinogenic drug ecstasy** was effective at treating symptoms of PTSD if administered by trained personnel along with psychotherapy.

- In one study, patients who received treatment for PTSD recovered almost **twice as fast** as those who received no treatment.

- Patients who appear to have completely recovered from PTSD can develop symptoms years later in response to **new traumas** or **significant events** such as the death of a loved one.

- A 2009 study of 55 combat veterans conducted by the Department of Defense found that **acupuncture** was more effective than medication and psychotherapy combined at treating PTSD.

- **Children** with PTSD should not be forced to talk about their trauma; instead, they should be encouraged to talk about it when they feel ready to.

- The treatment guidelines of the American Psychiatric Association and the Veterans Administration/Department of Defense recommend using both **psychotherapy and medication** to treat PTSD.

- Both the British and Australian government treatment guidelines recommend **psychotherapy** as the first-line treatment for PTSD; they recommend using medication only if therapy does not work or if the patient refuses therapy.

How Should Society Help Soldiers with Post-Traumatic Stress Disorder?

How Should Society Help Soldiers with Post-Traumatic Stress Disorder?

> **66 Ever since tribes of cavemen started throwing stones at each other, the wounds of war have been mental as well as physical. 99**
>
> —*Economist*, a British weekly newsmagazine.

> **66 Iraq has become a more effective incubator for post-traumatic stress disorder (PTSD) in the American service members than any mad scientist could possibly design. 99**
>
> —David L. Greenburg, a physician and public health expert in Washington, D.C., and Michael J. Roy, the director of the Division of Military Medicine and a professor of medicine at the Uniformed Services University in Bethesda, Maryland.

PTSD has long been associated with war. In fact, combat experience is the leading cause of PTSD among American men. A major study of U.S. veterans known as the National Vietnam Veterans Readjustment Study, conducted in 1990, estimated that 30.9 percent of Vietnam veterans would have PTSD at some point during their lives. In 2006 researchers reexamined the data from the study, focusing on veterans who were directly exposed to combat and using a narrower definition of PTSD. They concluded that a lower number—18.7 percent—of Vietnam veterans would suffer from war-related PTSD during their lives. This number, while lower than the original estimate, is still much higher than the lifetime rate of 7.8 percent among the general population.

Since early in the first decade of the 2000s, the United States has been involved in 2 major wars: Operation Enduring Freedom in Afghanistan, which began in October 2001, and Operation Iraqi Freedom in Iraq, which began in 2003. In 2008 the Rand Corporation, a highly regarded public policy research foundation, studied the extent of mental health problems among U.S. veterans of these wars. Rand questioned 1,965 soldiers and found that 14 percent had PTSD. This number is consistent with the results of other studies. It also coincides with a report from the army surgeon general showing that the number of soldiers diagnosed with PTSD increased 46 percent in 2007, reaching a 5-year total of 38,000.

The Challenges Faced by Today's Soldiers

The wars in Iraq and Afghanistan have placed heavy strains on American troops. As the Rand report notes, compared with previous wars, "deployments [to Iraq and Afghanistan] have been longer, redeployment to combat has been common, and breaks between deployments have been infrequent."[41] These long, frequent deployments make soldiers more prone to PTSD, since research shows that the disorder is more likely to afflict people subjected to prolonged and repeated trauma.

The situation on the ground in Iraq makes veterans of that war especially vulnerable. As stated by physicians David L. Greenburg and Michael J. Roy:

> The combat zone in Iraq has no frontline, no safe zone, and the embattled soldier has little with which to differentiate friend from foe, no warning of when the next improvised explosive device [bomb] will be detonated. It is hardly surprising that we are seeing high rates of depression, PTSD, and other anxiety disorders in service members who have been deployed to Iraq.[42]

Due to improvements in medical care and body armor, the casualty rates in the wars in Iraq and Afghanistan have been low relative to past wars. Many soldiers find themselves surviving situations that would have been fatal in previous wars. Although more are living through these horrific scenes of war, they are returning home with mental wounds, including traumatic memories and symptoms of PTSD.

Depression, TBI, and Suicide

In addition to PTSD, today's soldiers have other problems, and these conditions often overlap. The 2008 Rand study found that 14 percent of veterans from Iraq and Afghanistan have major depression. In addition, 19 percent—or 320,000—have traumatic brain injury (TBI), a form of brain damage that results from the blast of a nearby explosion, such as a roadside bomb. Symptoms of TBI can include headaches, dizziness, ringing in the ears, memory loss, and restlessness and agitation. Some symptoms of TBI are the same as those for PTSD, such as mood changes, difficulty concentrating, and sleep problems. These similarities in symptoms can make it hard to determine whether a veteran is suffering from TBI, PTSD, or both.

> **Combat experience is the leading cause of PTSD among American men.**

The burden of PTSD, along with other conditions such as TBI and depression, can make life extremely difficult for veterans. Along with symptoms of PTSD, veterans are also often overwhelmed with guilt due to their actions in combat and find it difficult to adjust from the high-adrenaline mind-set of soldiers to a more relaxed domestic pace of life at home. All these strains can lead to high rates of substance abuse, violence, and suicide. The Department of Defense reports that 140 active-duty soldiers committed suicide in 2008. For the first time the rate of suicide in the army exceeded the rate of the general population (19.5 per 100,000 versus 11 per 100,000). This is a surprising statistic, considering the fact that soldiers are screened for mental health problems before being accepted into the armed forces. While these suicides are not all attributable to PTSD, experts agree that PTSD is one factor driving more soldiers to take their own lives.

The Strain on Families

When a soldier returns from war with PTSD, the disorder takes a heavy toll on his or her family. Soldiers with PTSD often find it extremely difficult to reconnect with their families and resume their family roles as sons, daughters, husbands, wives, fathers, and mothers. Eric Goins, an Iraq war veteran, husband, and father of two boys, describes his difficulties after returning home with PTSD: "As far as our family relationship went, we didn't have one because I was either drunk or didn't want to talk. I just wanted to be alone. . . . I was pretty much scared to get back into life."[43] Colby Buzzell, another veteran of the Iraq war, describes how his marriage ended as a result of his PTSD: "My wife was the love of my life, the girl I wanted to spend the rest of my life with, but when I came back from Iraq, she was now a complete stranger to me, as I was to her. I couldn't relate to her, and she couldn't to me."[44]

Family members commonly say that the soldier who returns from war is not the same person who left. Symptoms of numbing and avoidance can be especially upsetting to husbands or wives, who often find their returning spouses transformed from warm, loving partners to cold, distant strangers. Spouses of soldiers with PTSD often find themselves struggling to keep their families together. Rebekah Benimoff, whose husband, Roger, served two tours of duty as an army chaplain in Iraq, describes the change she saw in her husband upon his return:

> Before long, Roger began acting strangely. He wouldn't stop exercising, as if he was running away from something. He wanted to eat only Special K and oatmeal, which meant we couldn't share a meal together as a family. We'd cuddle up in front of the TV, but then he'd jump off the couch to do hundreds of push-ups. He lost 30 pounds in two months. . . . He was "hypervigilant." . . . He suddenly couldn't stand crowds or noise. At times it seemed he couldn't stand people.[45]

Many spouses of soldiers develop their own mental health problems as they attempt to cope with their loved one's symptoms. Benimoff experienced a severe bout of depression, a common response. Others develop what is known as secondary PTSD. As explained by writer and army spouse Susan Nelson: "Secondary PTSD is the replication or the mirroring of some of the behaviors of an individual who has PTSD, due to close contact with the trauma survivor. It is the stress associated with trying to help a loved one who is suffering."[46]

The Benimoffs' marriage was severely tested, and they nearly divorced. Roger eventually received treatment for his PTSD but continued to struggle with symptoms. In the end, the Benimoffs managed to stay together, although their relationship had changed. As Rebekah explains, "I am learning to see him as a new Roger. Not the man I married. . . . He is a different person now, but he is reaching out. If I can join him . . . on his journey, I think our marriage will be stronger for it."[47] The Benimoffs' story is just one example of the stresses and strains that PTSD can put on a soldier's family.

Getting Treatment to Those Who Need It

The 2008 Rand study found that only about half of soldiers with PTSD seek treatment for the disorder. Many veterans are hesitant to reach out for help, for various reasons. One reason is the perceived stigma attached to having a mental disorder. This is especially true among military personnel, who are trained to be tough and who may see a mental problem as a sign of weakness. In addition, some soldiers fear that being diagnosed with a mental illness might prevent them from being redeployed or receiving promotions. Laurie B. Slone and Matthew J. Friedman explain the mind-set of a veteran who contemplates treatment for PTSD: "You may fear that if you admit to needing mental health assistance, you'll be ridiculed by your peers, seen as weak or cowardly, and considered unsuitable for military service because you weren't tough enough to 'suck it up.' . . . You may be afraid that seeking treatment will label you negatively and even damage your career."[48]

> " Along with symptoms of PTSD, veterans are also often overwhelmed with guilt due to their actions in combat and find it difficult to adjust from the high-adrenaline mind-set of soldiers to a more relaxed domestic pace of life at home. "

In addition to hesitancy on the part of veterans themselves, institutional barriers in the military and the Veterans Administration, the government agency responsible for caring for the nation's veterans, also prevent soldiers from getting good care. In fact, of those who do seek care, only about half get adequate treatment. This means that only about one-fourth of soldiers with PTSD are receiving the optimum care. One reason for this lack of quality care is a shortage of treatment professionals, which leaves many soldiers waiting a long time to be seen. As stated by Lawrence M. Wein, a professor of management science at Stanford University, "Those who seek follow-up treatment run into delays of up to 90 days."[49] Faced with such bureaucratic obstacles, many veterans who need help for their PTSD simply give up.

Many veterans advocates and political leaders are calling for improved treatment for soldiers with PTSD. They promote efforts to ease the stigma and fear associated with mental illness in the military and to remove the institutional barriers that keep so many veterans from seeking treatment. In addition, they advocate more funding in order to increase the number of mental health professionals and PTSD treatment programs. As stated in a 2008 editorial in the *St. Louis (MO) Post-Dispatch*:

> **Many spouses of soldiers develop their own mental health problems as they attempt to cope with their loved one's symptoms.**

> There's no excuse for the administration and Congress to not fully fund an intense mental health outreach program at the VA [Veterans Administration] and military base hospitals. Military commanders also must work to counteract the stigma attached to these unseen wounds. These soldiers and Marines have paid a heavy price while most of their fellow Americans have coasted. They deserve to be made whole.[50]

President Barack Obama has pledged to support the veterans of Iraq and Afghanistan and make sure they have the treatment they need. In a speech to the Veterans of Foreign Wars in August 2009, he stated:

> Post-Traumatic Stress and Traumatic Brain Injury are the defining injuries of today's wars. So caring for those affected by them is a defining purpose of my budget—billions of dollars more for treatment and mental health

screenings to reach our troops on the . . . frontlines and more mobile and rural clinics to reach veterans back home. We are not going to abandon these American heroes. We are going to do right by them.[51]

In addition to adding more money to the budget, Obama has taken steps to increase the size of the military in order to shorten the amount of time each soldier spends in combat zones.

Should Soldiers with PTSD Receive the Purple Heart?

In recent years some have advocated awarding soldiers with PTSD the Purple Heart, a medal typically given to soldiers who are wounded in combat. Advocates of extending the medal to PTSD sufferers argue that inner wounds experienced by those with PTSD are no less severe—and are sometimes more disabling—than many physical injuries. In short, they contend, the sacrifice that a PTSD sufferer has made for his or her country is as noble and as worthy of praise as the sacrifice made by a soldier who has taken fire. As stated by John Fortunato, a doctor and a Vietnam veteran who runs a PTSD treatment program for soldiers, "These guys have paid at least as high a price . . . as anybody with a traumatic brain injury [or] a shrapnel wound."[52]

> **In recent years some have advocated awarding soldiers with PTSD the Purple Heart, a medal typically given to soldiers who are wounded in combat.**

Opponents argue that awarding the Purple Heart to PTSD suffers would go against the original intent of the medal. As stated by Bob Mackey, a veteran of the first and second Iraq wars, "The Purple Heart was meant to be a badge of honor to show you were wounded in battle." He rejects the idea that psychological wounds are equivalent to physical wounds. "I've been in combat three times. There's stuff I've had to deal with. But it's substantially different from being physically hurt,"[53] he says. Other opponents point out the difficulty of diagnosing PTSD and the risk that the medal could be awarded to people who are faking or have been misdiagnosed.

In early 2009 the Department of Defense announced that the Purple Heart would not be extended to soldiers with PTSD. Explaining the decision, Department of Defense spokesperson Eileen Lainez said: "Historically, the Purple Heart has never been awarded for mental disorders or psychological conditions resulting from witnessing or experiencing traumatic combat events. Current medical knowledge and technologies do not establish PTSD as objectively and routinely as would be required for this award at this time."[54] Despite this decision, the debate over how to honor soldiers with PTSD—as well as how best to care for them when they return home—will no doubt continue.

How Should Society Help Soldiers with Post-Traumatic Stress Disorder?

66 **The Pentagon's recent decision not to award the Purple Heart to soldiers suffering from post-traumatic stress disorder strikes us as reasonable and well considered.** 99

—*New York Times*, "PTSD and the Purple Heart," January 12, 2009.

The *New York Times* is a nationally distributed New York newspaper.

66 **The Purple Heart ruling [the Pentagon's decision not to award the Purple Heart to soldiers with PTSD] is in keeping with . . . the official shortchanging of service members who were sent to fight.** 99

—Dan Rodricks, "Averting Their Eyes from Troops' Psychological Scars," *Baltimore Sun*, January 11, 2009.

Rodricks is a columnist for the *Baltimore Sun* newspaper.

Bracketed quotes indicate conflicting positions.

* Editor's Note: While the definition of a primary source can be narrowly or broadly defined, for the purposes of Compact Research, a primary source consists of: 1) results of original research presented by an organization or researcher; 2) eyewitness accounts of events, personal experience, or work experience; 3) first-person editorials offering pundits' opinions; 4) government officials presenting political plans and/or policies; 5) representatives of organizations presenting testimony or policy.

❝America's returning veterans of Operations Iraqi Freedom and Enduring Freedom are in the midst of the largest mental health crisis since the Vietnam War.❞

—Drew T. Doolin, "Healing Hidden Wounds: The Mental Health Crisis of America's Veterans," *Joint Force Quarterly,* July 2009.

Doolin is a colonel in the U.S. Marine Corps and a federal executive fellow at the Brookings Institution, a public policy research organization.

....

❝The high incidence of post-traumatic stress disorder (PTSD) among soldiers returning from Iraq is one of the many 'inconvenient truths' of this war.❞

—Judith D. Schwartz, "Treating the Trauma of War—Fairly," *Christian Science Monitor,* August 20, 2007.

Schwartz is a freelance writer with a master's degree in counseling psychology. Her work has appeared in the *Christian Science Monitor,* the *New York Times,* and many other publications.

....

❝He'd been back [from Iraq] for almost two months, but he was still checking to see where his weapon was every time he got in a vehicle. He drove aggressively, talked aggressively. . . . This was not the man I married, this hard-eyed, hyper-vigilant stranger.❞

—Stacy Bannerman, "Broken by This War," *Progressive,* March 2007.

Bannerman, an author, was the wife of an Army National Guard soldier who served in Iraq.

....

66 Even when treatment is available, service members often do not seek treatment, fearing it might damage their career or cause their peers to lose confidence in them. 99

—Arline Kaplan, "Untreated Vets: A 'Gathering Storm' of PTSD/Depression," *Psychiatric Times*, October 15, 2008.

Kaplan is a freelance writer who specializes in mental health topics.

66 All kidding aside, you can get terrifying PTSD just by walking into a VA [Veterans Administration] facility trying to get tested and/or treated for PTSD. 99

—Colby Buzzell, "Life After Wartime," *Esquire*, October 2007.

Buzzell is a veteran of the war in Iraq.

66 Left untreated, the soldier suffering from PTSD . . . can expect a lifetime of emotional struggles that will likely not resolve. Certainly, these soldiers deserve the very finest care our nation can provide. 99

—Kathy Platoni, "Healing on the Home Front," *Clinical Psychiatry News*, April 2007.

Platoni is a psychologist and a colonel in the U.S. Army.

❝However one feels about the nation's war policies, we have an ironclad obligation to look out for the short- and long-term needs of the troops we send off to combat.❞

—Bob Herbert, "Wounds You Can't See," *New York Times*, June 24, 2008.

Herbert is a columnist for the *New York Times*.

How Should Society Help Soldiers with Post-Traumatic Stress Disorder?

- About **30 percent** of cases of PTSD among U.S. citizens are caused by combat experience.

- The Rand Corporation estimates that **14 percent** of soldiers returning from Iraq and Afghanistan have PTSD.

- A study published in the *Archives of General Medicine* found that the rate of PTSD was **13 percent** among soldiers who had fought in Iraq and Afghanistan.

- The Department of Defense reports that the number of soldiers diagnosed with PTSD increased **46 percent** in 2007, for a 5-year total of 38,000.

- A study conducted by the U.S. Centers for Disease Control and Prevention found that veterans with **traumatic brain injury** face an increased risk of developing symptoms of PTSD.

- Research published in the *American Journal of Public Health* found that veterans **under the age of 25** had higher rates of PTSD than veterans over the age of 40.

- Only about **50 percent** of soldiers with PTSD or major depression seek mental health treatment, according to the Rand Corporation.

- The Veterans Administrations treats 200,000 people for PTSD each year at a cost of **$4 billion**.

- The Rand Corporation estimates that PTSD among veterans costs society between **$4 billion and $6.2 billion** over two years.

- A study published in the *Cochrane Database of Systematic Reviews* found that more than **50 percent** of soldiers with mental health problems thought they should handle the problem on their own.

Percentage of Iraq and Afghanistan Veterans with PTSD

Nearly 14 percent of the veterans of the war in Iraq, which began in 2003, and the war in Afghanistan, which began in 2001, have PTSD. Of those with PTSD, nearly three-fourths also have depression, traumatic brain injury (TBI), or both.

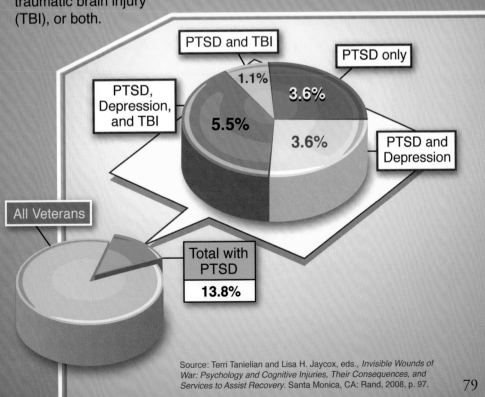

PTSD and TBI — 1.1%

PTSD only — 3.6%

PTSD, Depression, and TBI — 5.5%

PTSD and Depression — 3.6%

All Veterans

Total with PTSD — 13.8%

Source: Terri Tanielian and Lisa H. Jaycox, eds., *Invisible Wounds of War: Psychology and Cognitive Injuries, Their Consequences, and Services to Assist Recovery*. Santa Monica, CA: Rand, 2008, p. 97.

- A CBS News poll found that veterans between the ages of 20 and 24 are 2 to 4 times as likely to **commit suicide** as nonveterans in that age range.

- One study of Vietnam veterans found that those with PTSD had higher rates of **cardiovascular disease** than veterans without PTSD.

- A study published in August 2009 in the *Journal of Clinical Psychology* found that soldiers who served two **combat deployments** had a higher risk of PTSD than soldiers who served only one deployment.

New Cases of PTSD Among Soldiers

The number of new cases of PTSD among military personnel has increased dramatically since the start of the Iraq war in 2003. That year, 1,632 soldiers received a diagnosis of PTSD. Each subsequent year, the number of soldiers receiving a PTSD diagnosis has risen sharply. In 2007, the number of new cases was nearly 14,000, a 46 percent increase from the previous year and nearly ten times the number diagnosed in 2003.

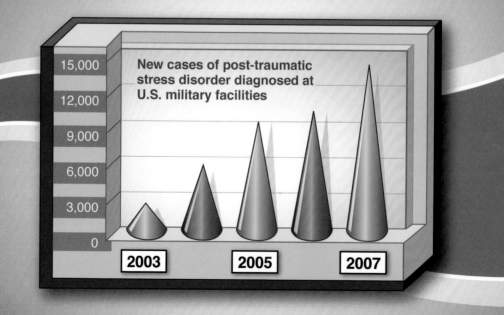

New cases of post-traumatic stress disorder diagnosed at U.S. military facilities

Source: Yochi J. Dreazen, "Number of Troops with Stress Disorder Rose 46% Last Year," *Wall Street Journal*, May 28, 2008, p.A2.

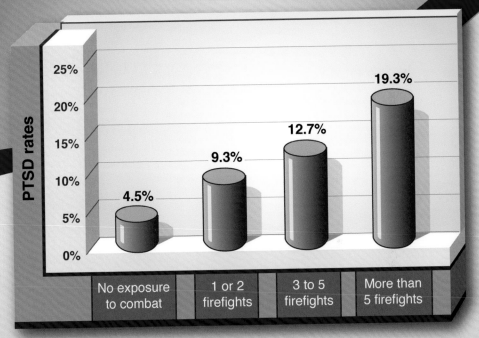

Rates of PTSD Increase with Exposure to Combat

Research among veterans from Iraq and Afghanistan shows that the more direct combat a soldier is exposed to, the greater likelihood that he or she will develop PTSD. Veterans who are involved in repeated firefights (exchanges of gunfire) are more likely to suffer from the disorder than those who are involved in one or fewer battles.

PTSD rates

- 4.5% — No exposure to combat
- 9.3% — 1 or 2 firefights
- 12.7% — 3 to 5 firefights
- 19.3% — More than 5 firefights

Source: John J. Spollen and Lawrence A. Labbate, "Posttraumatic Stress Disorder in Veterans," *Psychiatric Times*, February 2008, p. 37.

- The Veterans Administration runs a network of over 200 **PTSD treatment programs** and trauma centers, including both outpatient programs and inpatient programs ranging from 2 weeks to 90 days in length.

- A study of 272 soldiers who served in Iraq and Afghanistan found that those with **higher measures of psychological resilience and social support** were less likely to have PTSD than those with less resilience and social support.

The Symptoms of PTSD and TBI

Traumatic brain injury (TBI) is a type of brain damage that can result from the shock of nearby explosions. Many veterans of the war in Iraq experienced TBI as a result of the enemy's use of roadside bombs to attack troop convoys. Some of the effects, or symptoms, of TBI overlap with the symptoms of PTSD, making diagnosis and treatment of PTSD more difficult in veterans who have also suffered TBIs.

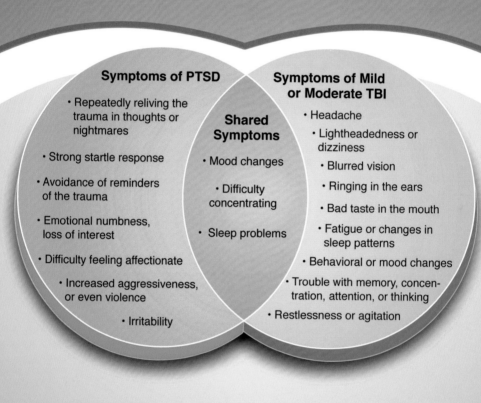

Symptoms of PTSD

- Repeatedly reliving the trauma in thoughts or nightmares
- Strong startle response
- Avoidance of reminders of the trauma
- Emotional numbness, loss of interest
- Difficulty feeling affectionate
- Increased aggressiveness, or even violence
- Irritability

Shared Symptoms

- Mood changes
- Difficulty concentrating
- Sleep problems

Symptoms of Mild or Moderate TBI

- Headache
- Lightheadedness or dizziness
- Blurred vision
- Ringing in the ears
- Bad taste in the mouth
- Fatigue or changes in sleep patterns
- Behavioral or mood changes
- Trouble with memory, concentration, attention, or thinking
- Restlessness or agitation

Source: Elise Foley and Hibah Yousuf, "A War at Home: Invisible Wounds, Big Costs," Medill on the Hill, March 16, 2009. http://medill.northwestern.edu.

- A study of soldiers who had served in Iraq found that those who reported **effective leadership and high unit cohesion** also reported less stigma regarding mental health issues and fewer barriers to treatment for mental illness.

Barriers to Treatment Among Today's Veterans

The Rand Corporation, a nonprofit research institute, questioned soldiers about their reasons for not seeking treatment for mental issues. The reason most frequently cited by veterans was the concern about the possible side effects of medication. Also top among the reasons were concerns about the effect of seeking treatment on one's career and on the perceptions of peers. Soldiers also indicated that they believed family and friends would be more helpful than mental health professionals.

Type of Barrier	Percentage
Logistical	
It would be difficult to get childcare or time off of work	29.3%
Mental health care would cost too much money	23.1%
It would be difficult to schedule an appointment	15.9%
I would not know where to get help or whom to see	15.9%
It would be difficult to arrange transportation to treatment	6.6%
Institutional and cultural	
It could harm my career	43.6%
I could be denied a security clearance in the future	43.6%
My coworkers would have less confidence in me if they found out	38.4%
I do not think my treatment would be kept confidential	29.0%
My commander or supervisor might respect me less	23.0%
My friends and family would respect me less	11.5%
I could lose contact or custody of my children	9.3%
My commander or supervisor has asked us not to get treatment	7.8%
My spouse or partner would not want me to get treatment	2.9%
Beliefs and preferences for treatment	
The medications that might help have too many side effects	45.1%
My family or friends would be more helpful than a mental health professional	39.4%
I would think less of myself if I could not handle it on my own	29.1%
Religious counseling would be more helpful than mental health treatment	28.8%
Even good mental health care is not very effective	25.2%
The mental health treatments available to me are not very good	24.6%
I have received treatment before and it did not work	18.0%

Note: Numbers in this table do not add up to 100 percent because respondents were allowed to choose as many answers as they considered relevant.

Source: Terri Tanielian and Lisa H. Jaycox, eds., *Invisible Wounds of War: Psychological and Cognitive Injuries, Their Consequences, and Services to Assist Recovery.* Santa Monica, CA: Rand, 2008, p. 104.

Key People and Advocacy Groups

Naomi Breslau: A professor of epidemiology at Michigan State University and a prominent PTSD researcher who has investigated the prevalence of the disorder in urban areas.

Edna B. Foa: A professor of clinical psychology in psychiatry at the University of Pennsylvania and the director of the Center for the Treatment and Study of Anxiety, Foa has been the lead researcher on many studies on psychotherapy treatments for PTSD.

Matthew J. Friedman: The executive director of the U.S. Department of Veterans Affairs National Center for Post-Traumatic Stress Disorder and a professor of psychiatry at Dartmouth Medical School. He has been the lead researcher on many studies on PTSD as well as the author of numerous books on the topic.

Ira Hayes: A World War II veteran who was among the men who famously raised the American flag on Iwo Jima. It is speculated that he suffered from PTSD after the war.

Iraq and Afghanistan Veterans of America: An advocacy group that works on behalf of the veterans of the wars in Iraq and Afghanistan and their families, including those with PTSD.

Ronald C. Kessler: A professor of health care policy at Harvard Medical School, Kessler is the lead investigator of the National Comorbidity Survey, the largest study of the prevalence of mental illness—including PTSD—in the United States.

Richard A. Kulka: The senior research vice president at the Research Triangle Institute, a nonprofit research organization that conducts research for both business and government clients. He was the lead researcher of the landmark National Vietnam Veterans Readjustment Study, the first government-sponsored study of PTSD.

Military Families Speak Out: An organization of more than 3,400 families opposed to the wars in Iraq and Afghanistan who have relatives or loved ones who are currently in the military or who have served in the military since November 2002. Among other causes, the group advocates more support for troops with PTSD.

National Alliance on Mental Illness: Formerly the National Alliance for the Mentally Ill, a nonprofit organization that works to improve the lives of people with mental illnesses, including PTSD, by means of education and advocacy.

Herold Noel: An Iraq war veteran and father of three who came back from the war with PTSD and ended up homeless. He was featured in the 2006 documentary *When I Came Home* about homeless veterans and the perceived failure of the Veterans Administration to help them.

Joshua Omvig: An army reservist who returned from Iraq with PTSD and committed suicide in 2005 at the age of 22. His death led to congressional legislation in his name creating a program to prevent suicide among soldiers. The Joshua Omvig Veterans Suicide Prevention Act was signed into law in 2007.

Roger Pitman: A professor of psychiatry at Harvard Medical School and an internationally recognized researcher, teacher, and clinician focusing on PTSD. He is the lead researcher in a study to determine whether the drugs known as beta-blockers can help prevent PTSD.

Barry Roma: A Vietnam veteran who developed PTSD and became an antiwar activist and a member of Vietnam Veterans Against the War.

Vietnam Veterans of America: A congressionally chartered nonprofit organization that supports Vietnam veterans. Its PTSD/Substance Abuse Committee advocates increased health care for veterans with PTSD, substance addictions, and other psychological reactions to trauma resulting from military service.

Chronology

1980

The term *post-traumatic stress disorder* is officially recognized for the first time when the condition is included as an anxiety disorder in the third edition of the *DSM*. PTSD is defined as a stress reaction to an event falling "outside the range of usual human experience."

1861–1865

During the American Civil War, soldiers who display symptoms of what is now known as post-traumatic stress disorder (PTSD) are said to have "soldier's heart" or "irritable heart."

1952

The first edition of the *Diagnostic and Statistical Manual of Mental Disorders (DSM)*, the American Psychiatric Association's (APA) catalog of mental illnesses, includes the diagnosis "gross stress reaction" for symptoms resulting from stress, including combat-induced stress.

1860   1890   1920   1950   1980

1968

The second edition of the *DSM* is published without the "gross stress reaction" diagnosis.

1914–1918

Horrific conditions of trench warfare during World War I leave many veterans with PTSD, then known as "shell shock" due to the mistaken belief that it is caused by changes in air pressure resulting from exploding artillery shells.

1939–1945

Many veterans of World War II return with PTSD, then labeled "combat fatigue."

1972

The *New York Times* publishes an op-ed article entitled "Post-Vietnam Syndrome," in which psychologist Chaim Shatan describes symptoms of what will later be called PTSD among Vietnam veterans. The term *post-Vietnam syndrome* becomes the newest label for PTSD among veterans.

1983
Congress mandates an investigation into the rates of PTSD among Vietnam veterans, launching the landmark National Vietnam Veterans Readjustment Study. The results are published in 1990.

2008
The U.S. Army's surgeon general announces that the number of new PTSD diagnoses among military personnel increased tenfold between 2003 and 2007, reaching a total of 38,000 new cases.

1990
Researchers begin the National Comorbidity Survey, the first survey of the rate of PTSD among the general population in the United States.

2005
On the American Gulf Coast, high rates of PTSD are left in the wake of Hurricane Katrina. The rates remain high for years, due to the slow pace of recovery.

1985   1990   1995   2000   2005

1994
In the fourth edition of the *DSM*, the APA removes the stipulation that the stressor causing PTSD must fall "outside the range of usual human experience," an acknowledgment that the types of traumas that cause PTSD are relatively common.

2009
The Department of Defense announces that it will not award the Purple Heart to soldiers with PTSD.

2001
In the aftermath of the September 11, 2001, terrorist attacks, the rate of PTSD rises to as high as 20 percent near ground zero. However, the rate returns to normal within a few months as the community pulls together and rebuilds.

Related Organizations

African American Post Traumatic Stress Disorder Association (AAPTSDA)
9129 Veterans Dr. SW
Lakewood, WA 98498
phone: (253) 589-0766
fax: (253) 589-0769
e-mail: tacomaptsd@earthlink.net
Web site: www.aaptsdassn.org

The AAPTSDA is a nonprofit organization that seeks to educate the public, improve treatment programs, and provide direct services to veterans with PTSD. It is committed to helping all veterans—not just minorities—receive the treatments and Veterans Administration benefits they need. It publishes a monthly newsletter and maintains a Web site that contains information about PTSD and its treatments as well as links to many resources for veterans with PTSD and their families.

American Psychiatric Association (APA)
1000 Wilson Blvd., Suite 1825
Arlington, VA 22209-3901
phone: (703) 907-7300; toll-free: (888) 357-7924
e-mail: apa@psych.org
Web site: www.psych.org

The APA is a medical specialty society composed primarily of psychiatrists or people working to become psychiatrists. It strives to ensure humane care and effective treatment for all persons with mental disorders. The APA publishes the *Diagnostic and Statistical Manual of Mental Disorders*, the psychiatric profession's primary reference book for the diagnosis and treatment of mental illness, as well as the monthly *American Journal of Psychiatry*, the bimonthly *Psychiatric News*, and various books and reports.

American Psychological Association
750 First St. NE
Washington, DC 20002-4242

phone: (202) 336-5500; toll-free: (800) 374-2721
e-mail: public.affairs@apa.org
Web site: www.apa.org

The American Psychological Association, the largest association of psychologists worldwide, is a scientific and professional organization that represents psychology in the United States. It seeks to increase understanding, improve treatments, and educate the public about mental illnesses by means of research, training, and advocacy. It publishes the bimonthly *Monitor on Psychology* as well as various books, journals, and newsletters. Its Web site includes a section devoted to the topic of PTSD.

Anxiety Disorders Association of America (ADAA)

8730 Georgia Ave., Suite 600
Silver Spring, MD 20910
phone: (240) 485-1001
fax: (240) 485-1035
e-mail: amuskin@adaa.org
Web site: www.adaa.org

The ADAA is a nonprofit organization dedicated to informing the public, health care professionals, and the media about anxiety disorders—including PTSD. It seeks to increase knowledge about causes and treatment of anxiety disorders, assist people with anxiety disorders in finding appropriate treatment, and reduce the stigma surrounding anxiety disorders. The ADAA publishes the *Triumph* newsletter and offers information about PTSD and other topics on its Web site.

Department of Veterans Affairs (VA)

810 Vermont Ave. NW
Washington, DC 20420
phone: (800) 827-1000
Web site: www.va.gov

The VA is the department of the federal government responsible for caring for the nation's 25 million military veterans. The Veterans Health Administration, an organization within the VA, provides health benefits and services to veterans who have been injured or have suffered mental illness as a result of serving their country. The VA's National Center for Post-Traumatic Stress Disorder works to improve the care of veterans with PTSD through research, education, and training. It offers information about PTSD on its Web site (www.ptsd.va.gov).

Gift from Within (GFW)

16 Cobb Hill Rd.
Camden, ME 04843
phone: (207) 236-8858
fax: (207) 236-2818
e-mail: joyceb3955@aol.com
Web site: www.giftfromwithin.org

GFW is a nonprofit organization that offers support and counseling to victims of post-traumatic stress disorder. It develops and disseminates educational materials, including videotapes, articles, and books, and maintains a roster of survivors who are willing to participate in an international network of peer support.

Institute of Medicine (IOM)

500 Fifth St. NW
Washington, DC 20001
phone: (202) 334-2352
fax: (202) 334-1412
e-mail: iomwww@nas.edu
Web site: www.iom.edu

The IOM, a division of the National Academy of Sciences, is a nonprofit organization chartered to provide the nation with science-based advice on matters of biomedical science, medicine, and health. The institute works outside the framework of government to ensure scientifically informed analysis and independent guidance. It publishes the reports *Posttraumatic Stress Disorder: Diagnosis and Assessment; Treatment of PTSD: An Assessment of the Evidence;* and *Gulf War and Health,* Vol. 6: *Physiologic, Psychologic, and Psychosocial Effects of Deployment Related Stress.*

International Society for Traumatic Stress Studies (ISTSS)

111 Deer Lake Rd., Suite 100
Deerfield, IL 60015
phone: (847) 480-9028

fax: (847) 480-9282
e-mail: istss@istss.org
Web site: www.istss.org

The ISTSS is a professional membership organization that promotes the spread of knowledge about severe stress and trauma. The society seeks to increase understanding of the scope and consequences of traumatic exposure, prevent traumatic events and ameliorate their consequences, and provide advocacy for the field of traumatic stress. It publishes the *Journal of Traumatic Stress* and the quarterly newsletter *Traumatic StressPoints* and develops and promotes treatment guidelines for PTSD.

National Child Traumatic Stress Network (NCTSN)

NCCTS—University of California, Los Angeles
11150 W. Olympic Blvd., Suite 650
Los Angeles, CA 90064
phone: (310) 235-2633
fax: (310) 235-2612
e-mail: info@nctsnet.org
Web site: www.nctsnet.org

The NCTSN is a nonprofit organization created by Congress to raise the standard of care and increase access to services for traumatized children and their families across the United States. It serves as a national resource for developing and providing interventions, services, and public and professional education. The NCTSN publishes fact sheets, FAQs, and brochures on issues related to childhood stress and its treatment.

National Institute of Mental Health (NIMH)

Science Writing, Press, and Dissemination Branch
6001 Executive Blvd., Room 8184, MSC 9663
Bethesda, MD 20892-9663
phone: (301) 443-4513; toll-free (866) 615-6464
fax: (301) 443-4279
e-mail: nimhinfo@nih.gov
Web site: www.nimh.nih.gov

Part of the National Institutes of Health, the NIMH is a department of the federal government responsible for conducting research into the causes, treatments, and cures of mental illnesses. It publishes fact sheets, booklets, and pamphlets for the general public on PTSD and how to get help and assist others who are experiencing symptoms of the disorder. Titles include *Post-Traumatic Stress Disorder* and *Helping Children and Adolescents Cope with Violence and Disasters: What Parents Can Do.*

Sidran Institute

200 E. Joppa Rd., Suite 207
Baltimore, MD 21286-3107
phone: (410) 825-8888
fax: (410) 337-0747
e-mail: info@sidran.org
Web site: www.sidran.org

The Sidran Institute is a nonprofit organization that helps people understand, recover from, and treat the emotional and spiritual injuries—including PTSD—that result from traumatic events. It develops and delivers educational programming; resources for treatment, support, and self-help; and publications about trauma and recovery. Publications include the fact sheet "Myths and Facts About PTSD," the brochure *What Is Post-Traumatic Stress Disorder?* and the book *Back from the Front: Combat Trauma, Love, and the Family.*

For Further Research

Books

Victoria Lemle Beckner and John B. Arden, *Conquering Post-Traumatic Stress Disorder: The Newest Techniques for Overcoming Symptoms, Regaining Hope, and Getting Your Life Back.* Beverly, MA: Far Winds, 2008.

Penny Coleman, *Flashback: Posttraumatic Stress Disorder, Suicide, and the Lessons of War.* Boston: Beacon, 2006.

Kendall Johnson, *After the Storm: Healing After Trauma, Tragedy and Terror.* Alameda, CA: Hunter House, 2006.

Monique Lang, *Healing from Post-Traumatic Stress.* New York: McGraw-Hill, 2007.

Aphrodite Matsakis, *Back from the Front: Combat Trauma, Love, and the Family.* Baltimore, MD: Sidran, 2007.

Ilona Meagher, *Moving a Nation to Care: Post-Traumatic Stress Disorder and America's Returning Troops.* Brooklyn, NY: Ig, 2007.

Richard F. Mollica, *Healing Invisible Wounds: Paths to Hope and Recovery in a Violent World.* Orlando, FL: Harcourt, 2006.

Daryl S. Paulson and Stanley Krippner, *Haunted by Combat: Understanding PTSD in War Veterans Including Women, Reservists, and Those Coming Back from Iraq.* Westport, CT: Praeger, 2007.

Glen Schiraldi, *The Post-Traumatic Stress Disorder Sourcebook: A Guide to Healing, Recovery, and Growth.* 2nd ed. New York: McGraw-Hill, 2009.

Laurie B. Slone and Matthew J. Friedman, *After the War Zone: A Practical Guide for Returning Troops and Their Families.* Philadelphia: Da Capo, 2008.

Clint Van Winkle, *Soft Spots: A Marine's Memoir of Combat and Post-Traumatic Stress Disorder.* New York: St. Martin's, 2009.

Periodicals

Matt Bean, "When Memories Are Scars," *Men's Health*, November 2006.

Rebekah Benimoff, "A Story of Love, War, and Faith," *Redbook*, March 2009.

Tyler E. Boudreau, "Troubled Minds and Purple Hearts," *New York Times*, January 26, 2009.

Colby Buzzell, "Life After Wartime,*" Esquire*, October 2007.

Eve Conant, "To Share in the Horror," *Newsweek*, March 19, 2007.

Yochi J. Dreazen, "Number of Troops with Stress Disorder Rose 46% Last Year," *Wall Street Journal*, May 28, 2008.

Marilyn Elias, "Trauma Shapes Katrina's Kids," *USA Today*, August 16, 2007.

Melissa Healy, "Tetris to Ease War Anguish?" *Los Angeles Times*, January 10, 2009.

Gordon Lubold, "Army Uses Video Games in Suicide Prevention," *Christian Science Monitor*, November 26, 2008.

Richard Ransley, "PTSD Comes in Many Forms," *Santa Fe New Mexican*, June 3, 2007.

Sally Satel, "A Helping Hand for Vets," *Wall Street Journal*, February 26, 2008.

Chandra R. Thomas, "The Storm Within," *Essence*, September 2008.

Mark Thompson, "Death at the Army's Hands," *Time*, February 25, 2008.

Washington Times, "Military Spouses Also Suffer Severe Stress," July 2, 2009.

Lawrence M. Wein, "Counting the Walking Wounded," *New York Times*, January 26, 2009.

Christopher Werth, "A Violent Virtual Cure," *Newsweek International*, November 17, 2008.

David Zucchino, "For Parents, Their Own Trauma," *Los Angeles Times*, December 14, 2008.

Internet Sources

Tori DeAngelis, "PTSD Treatments Grow in Evidence, Effectiveness," *Monitor on Psychology*, January 2008. www.apa.org/monitor/jan08/ptsd.html.

Mike A. Glasch, "Battling PTSD," *Soldiers*, August 2007. www.army.mil/publications/soldiersmagazine/pdfs/aug07all.pdf.

Mayo Clinic Staff, "Post-Traumatic Stress Disorder (PTSD)," April 10, 2009. www.mayoclinic.com/health/post-traumatic-stress-Disorder/DS00246.

Medline Plus, "PTSD: A Growing Epidemic," Winter 2009. www.nlm.nih.gov/medlineplus/magazine/issues/winter09/articles/winter09pg10-14.html.

National Institute of Mental Health, "Post-Traumatic Stress Disorder (PTSD)," 2008. www.nimh.nih.gov/health/publications/post-traumatic-stress-disorder-ptsd/index.shtml.